Dedicated to
Śri Kṛiṣṇa Pattabhi Jois,
"Guruji"

Acknowledgments

Thanks go to a number of people who have endeavoured to keep this edition on track.
To the garage girls: Tiffany Fleetwood-Bird, Lesley Cargill and Jeni Caffin.
Also to Brendan Healey, Jenny Porter, Ann Sweeney, Jean Byrne and Robert Schutze.

Lastly, thanks and praise to K. P. Jois.
None of this would have been possible without his dedication to yoga.

Photographs by Gilles Vancoillie and Mark Gerritsen.
Artwork by Tiffany Fleetwood-Bird and Matthew Sweeney.
Printed by Bangkok Post 2005.

First edition printed 2002.
Second edition printed 2003.
Third edition printed 2005.

The practices displayed in this book should only be undertaken with the guidance of an experienced teacher or, where appropriate, a qualified medical practitioner.

THE YOGA TEMPLE

e-mail: yogatemple@hotmail.com
www.yogatemple.com

CONTENTS

INTRODUCTION

ĀSANA & VINYĀSA

Introduction

Aṣṭāṅga vinyāsa yoga is a system of postures connected by the breath. It combines sequential, flowing movements with focused internal awareness. Through self practice and self observation a non-judgmental attitude is cultivated. This peaceful quality is manifested by focusing on the flowing nature of the breath. The breath is the vehicle by which the body and mind are observed, purified and transcended.

Aṣṭāṅga Yoga As It Is provides an exploration of both the physical and mental aspects of the *Aṣṭāṅga yoga* practice. The following introduction attempts to shed light on some core *yoga* concepts and relevant self development principles. The photographic section depicts both the *āsana* of the traditional sequences and all of the relevant *vinyāsa*. However, this book is not a "how to do it" manual. It does cover the main points of the tradition including many of the unwritten rules that dominate the Mysore-method. I have attempted to expand on why these rules are important, including the benefits of the traditional practice and also some of the possible drawbacks. In order for an individual to integrate the tradition a complete therapeutic and holistic approach is also necessary. Some criticisms can be made in order to understand the practice in terms of *yoga* rather than merely *āsana*. *As It Is* aims to promote a questioning attitude to the practice, to help examine and integrate many of its qualities. As the physical practice evolves there should be a natural and healthy interest in the mental and emotional processes that go with it.

The text uses a number of phrases in Sanskrit. It is helpful to understand a little of this language as it adds depth to the practice and a personal connection to the living history of *yoga*. Where possible the most accurate use of Sanskrit to English transliteration has been used. None of the material in this book is new, I merely present it in my own fashion.

Om Śanti
Matthew Sweeney

Śri K.P. Jois

Any introduction to the practice of *Aṣṭāṅga yoga* should mention Śri Kriṣṇa Pattabhi Jois and his cultivation of the *vinyāsa* method. He is affectionately called Guruji by his students. The meaning for *guru* is heavy one, someone replete with the weight of *yoga*. Born in 1915, K.P. Jois' introduction to *yoga* began at the age of twelve with Śri T. Kriṣṇamacharya, with whom he studied from 1927 to 1945. He studied *Sanskrit sahitya veda* and *advaita vedanta* in the Mysore Maharaja Sanskrit College from 1930 to 1956. In 1937 he was elected Professor and Head of Department and was honoured by the title *Yogāsana Viśarada* by Śri Jagadguru Śankaracharya of Puri in 1945. In 1948 he established the *Aṣṭāṅga Yoga Nilayam* in Mysore, India, to practice, refine and teach this method. Many students have since come to Mysore, bringing *Aṣṭāṅga yoga* to most parts of the world.

For many years Guruji taught from a small room in the downstairs area of his house, the *Nilayam* in Lakshmipuram, Mysore. This room could hold a maximum of twelve students with a bare hand-span between their mats: five students in front, five in the back, and two sideways, facing each other in the middle. If one had a loose practice it became

phrase "Mysore-style" was coined. Starting at about 5am the first set of twelve students would begin their practice. They would repeat the prayer after Guruji and then start *Sūryanamsakara A*. Once finished back bending and receiving a squash in *Paśchimottānāsana* from the *guru* the student would be sent upstairs to do the finishing sequence on his or her own. Depending on the length of the practice the student could be anywhere from half an hour to two hours in the downstairs *śala*. Other students would then be waiting on the stairs until their spot became available and Guruji called them down, "Yes, yes! You come!"

Any adjustment received from Guruji could be a life-changing and cathartic experience. Upon Guruji's approach, this usually quiet and unassuming man of below average height suddenly becomes a giant, the weight of over seventy years of *yoga* behind him. Despite the seeming grumpiness, his comments of "bad lady!" or "bad man!" came with a smile. As one female student confronted him: "I have discovered your secret Guruji. 'Bad lady' really means 'good lady'." "Oh, haha," he laughed, "Smart lady."

Author and fellow students chanting the prayer with Guruji and his grandson Sharath, Mysore, November 1995.

The Mysore self-practice is unique compared to other *āsana* classes. You practice at your own pace, by and large without interruption. There could be occasional comments from Guruji, such as, "Put it your head down!" or "No, No! Grab it your foot fingers!" or more rarely "Uh... correct." There is little noise except for deep breathing and the occasional grunt. Mysore-style practice has both an intense quality and a quality of inward looking, of meditation. You simply do your practice, receive certain adjustments and wait for the next posture. Sometimes it is a long wait.

Some students would come to Mysore, saying they were doing Intermediate and some Advanced, only to find that with Guruji half of the Primary sequence was where they were stopped. Guruji would not allow a student to progress without being able to successfully complete every posture. Frustrating for some, educational for others. It all depended on your mind-set. (See page 8 for further details of this aspect of the tradition.) Another potentially frustrating element was the hierarchy of the stairs. Guruji would often reserve a spot for a long term student, or a student would jump the queue and simply grab the spot they wanted. There were many disgruntled stair-waiters. In the end it never

Śri T. Kṛiṣṇamacharya

Professor Śri Trimulai Kṛiṣṇamacharya is considered by many to be the grandfather of modern *yoga*. By and large it is through his teachings that the systems of *Aṣṭāṅga yoga* (K.P. Jois), *Iyengar yoga* (B.K.S. Iyengar) and *Vini yoga* (T.K.V. Desikachar) were each developed. In the early years of his teaching Kṛiṣṇamacharya used the *vinyāsa krama* method, that of linking postures together in sequence by numbers. (Now called *Aṣṭāṅga vinyāsa yoga* by K.P. Jois.)

Later Kṛiṣṇamacharya reportedly discovered a copy of the "*Yoga Korunta*" in Calcutta University, an ancient text written by Ṛiṣi Vamana. It was a confirmation of the *vinyāsa* method. Apparently Kṛiṣṇamacharya used the book to solidify his understanding of *vinyāsa*. However, as there is no modern form of this book it is not possible to verify its legitimacy. It seems to have passed with Kṛiṣṇamacharya. Written evidence or not, the proof of the benefits are in the practice.

As time passed Śri T. Kṛiṣṇamacharya developed and refined his teaching with different methods for different individuals. As well as the *vinyāsa krama*, he used specific props for therapeutic purposes and he advocated individual *yoga* programs, one-on-one tuition with gentle *prāṇāyāma* being introduced from the start. Family life was important to Kṛiṣṇamacharya, so much so that he refused the honour of becoming Head *Swami* of the *Parakala Math*, a respected lineage. His reply to each of the three times that he was asked was that he wished to spend time with his family. As *brahmacharya* or monk-like celibacy is considered ideal for yoga practice, this view of Kṛiṣṇamacharya's was remarkable.

At one time Kṛiṣṇamacharya demonstrated his *siddhis*, or abilities, for the Maharaja of Mysore, who was also one of his students. He had wires attached to his head and the electric light switch and turned the palace lights on and off. At another time in the 1930s, with a foreign medical team in attendance, he stopped his heart for a full two minutes. Although these abilities may seem an attractive incentive for doing *yoga*, for this *yogācharya* they were merely the bi-product of many years of practice, not the goal. It was only after practicing for over twenty-five years that Kṛiṣṇamacharya began to teach *yoga*. T.K.V. Desikachar describes his father's practice when Kṛiṣṇamacharya was over ninety:

> Whether you believe it or not, this old man gets up at one o'clock in the morning... He practices his *yogāsana* and *prāṇāyāma* every day... And at five o'clock the bell rings and we know he has started his *puja*... He makes his own breakfast. Then I go to see him at seven o'clock in the morning and we chant for one hour.
>
> *The Yoga of T. Kṛiṣṇamacharya*

Kṛiṣṇamacharya's teacher was Rāmamohana Brahmachārī. He lived with his teacher for over seven years learning *āsana* and *vinyāsa* practice, *yoga* therapy and *yoga* philosophy. Kṛiṣṇamacharya passed away in 1989 at the age of one-hundred. Beyond these scant details it is impossible to further track the history of the living *vinyāsa* method. Most of the older tradition (some say stemming back to Patañjāli) is unverifiable and largely based on hearsay and conjecture.

The Practice: *Ujjāyi Prāṇāyāma*

The starting point for any *āsana* practice is the breath and for *Aṣṭāṅga yoga* the starting point of the breath is *ujjāyi prāṇāyāma*. *Ujjāyi* is defined as extended victory. *Prāṇa* is variously defined as "breath, respiration, wind, life force, life, energy, strength, the hidden energy in the atmospheric air." *Prāṇāyāma* is most clearly defined as the development *(āyāma)* of life-energy *(prāṇa)* rather than the restraint *(yama)* of breath *(prāṇa)*. The breath is the first component of the *tristhānaṁ*, or three places of attention. It is through the breath that the other two components, the body and mind are transformed.

> Respiration being disturbed, the mind becomes disturbed. By restraining respiration, the *yogi* gets steadiness of mind. So long as the (breathing) air stays in the body, it is called life. Death consists in the passing out of the (breathing) air... *Ujjāyi*: having closed the opening of the larynx, the air should be drawn in such a way that it goes touching from the throat to the chest and making a noise while passing.
>
> *The Haṭha Yoga Pradipīka,* 2: 2, 3, 51.

By gently contracting the glottis area at the back of the throat, one can breathe in a controlled manner. This contraction creates a deep, sonorous sound, which increases the movement of the diaphragm and lengthens the spine. Initially, the sound of the breath may be a little exaggerated and raspy by over squeezing the glottis, eventually becoming both soft and steady. A soft, consistent sound aids the consistent flow of breath and helps to build heat in the body, ideal for any *āsana* practice. The heat produced is not only conducive for stretching, but cleans and purifies the body through the sweat. It should be noted that the breath should be as gentle as possible to keep it natural and organic. Avoid being forceful, otherwise this imposition will develop constraints rather than freedoms.

In *yogic* physiology the sun represents the fire element in the body, the inhalation (*pūraka*), the heart and the life force. The moon represents the cooling element, the exhalation (*rechaka*), the lungs and the death force. By controlling the breathing, one inhibits the death force. The fire, *agni*, increases and the life force increases. *Ujjāyi prāṇāyāma* is the victory of life.

There are three main areas where the sound of the breath resonates: the nostrils, the palate, and the throat (Figure 1). Only when the sound is at the back of the throat can it begin to resonate in the chest cavity, giving the diaphragm full range of movement.

Experiment with the following exercises:

1. First breathe through the nose and accentuate the breath there. Flare the nostrils. The breath sounds quite airy. There is a common tendency to either gasp the air in with the nose, or through inattention not realise that this sound is in the nose and is not traveling to the throat and chest. This indicates a state of unconsciousness or lack of awareness and is more common on the inhalation.

2. Clench the teeth and try to use the *ujjāyi* breath. With the jaw locked, the sound hisses inside the mouth and bounces off the upper palate. When particularly tense in an *āsana* there is often an unnecessary reflection of this tension in the jaw and face. This indicates a state of hyper-tension, or awareness that is pushy and fixed and is more common on the exhalation.

3. Drop the lower jaw, creating a sizeable gap between the upper and lower teeth and again create the *ujjāyi* sound. With the face relaxed in this way the sound becomes smoother, softer, more resonant and less harsh. Focus both the exhalation and the inhalation with the jaw dropped and the face relaxed. The feeling is a little like breathing through the ears: the inner ear presses, and the cavern of the skull echoes with the sound. The mind becomes empty.

Figure 1.

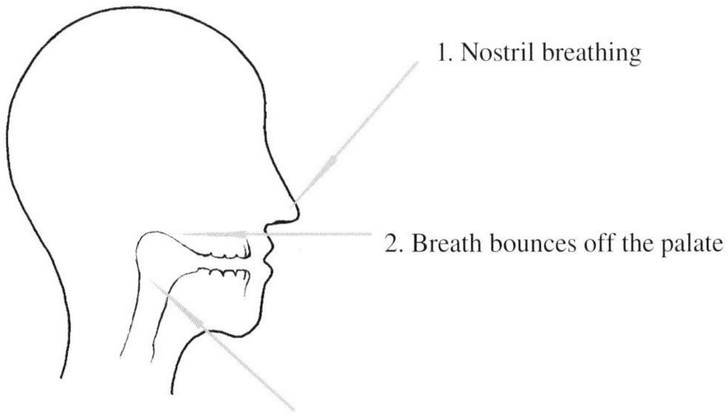

There is a direct relationship between dropping the lower jaw (softly increasing the *ujjāyi* sound), lengthening the spine and the freedom of movement of the diaphragm. That is, the correct application of the *ujjāyi* restriction at the base of the throat subtly activates the *jālandhara bandha,* increasing the *uḍḍīyāna bandha* diaphragmatic movement. The *uḍḍīyāna* likewise increases the rising *mūla bandha*. The flowing process of *ujjāyi prāṇāyāma* promotes all three *bandha* equally. See the *bandha* section (page 14) for more details.

It is common for the sound of the breath to be louder and longer on the exhalation, and quieter and shorter on the inhalation. Try to balance the breathing between lack of awareness (exercise one) and fixed awareness (exercise two). Generally the sound of the inhalation should be increased, or more sound through the base of the throat, and the sound of the exhalation should be more relaxed, or softer sound through the base of the throat. With the *ujjāyi* sound consistent, the breathing lengthens evenly throughout the practice. Awareness of your body's needs of the moment will increase and injury will be unlikely. A combination of inattention and facial contortion causes most injuries. If the breathing is both soft and secure it is almost impossible to push too hard. Do not push if the breathing becomes secondary to achieving a posture. If the face stays relaxed, the breathing naturally becomes softer. It is not necessary for the whole room to shake when you maintain *ujjāyi*! Experienced practitioners generally have much quieter breathing.

For beginners it is normal and useful to emphasise the exhalation and the *ujjāyi* sound on exhalation: to let go, extend and breathe out for longer. For more experienced students, it is also helpful to emphasise the out-breath when learning a new, unfamiliar *āsana*. There is a natural tendency for the inhalation to be shorter than the exhalation, particularly with upward dog, other back arching movements and twists. When the diaphragm is restricted by a posture, try to keep the start of the inhalation soft and subtle, rather than abrupt. When out of breath the inhalation is often drawn in too quickly out of panic, further aggravating the tension. Relax what is possible to relax and the breath and body will then be harmonious.

One way to facilitate the extension of the inhalation in all *āsana* is to count the breath. For example, inhale for a count of five and exhale for a count of five. At a certain point, however, this type of practice becomes laborious, particularly if maintained for the whole sequence. It can also take you away from the natural tendency of the breath, become too much of a physical strain and be potentially injurious. Lengthening the inhalation increases the fiery nature of the practice, produces greater sweat, with the exhalation removing toxins. The inhalation brings energy (tension) in, the exhalation releases it.

It should be noted that the air one draws in is not strictly speaking *prāṇa*. The inhalation brings in both air *and prāṇa*. *Prāṇa* is the vital, life-giving aspect of the incoming air, not the whole thing. The air portion often has a degree of toxicity, various forms of physical or energetic pollution. The exhalation removes this toxicity, but also pushes out *prāṇa* and energy is depleted. As the breathing becomes more refined, improving the individual's boundaries, the system *only* takes in that which is nourishing and rejects *only* that which is toxic. Also, it may be said that the practice of *prāṇāyāma* does not actually increase energy. It is awareness of *prāṇa* that is already there that increases. It is accessing your full potential that is difficult.

If the inhalation brings excessive tension with it, then a more relaxed breath will be necessary. The breath should always be flowing. By avoiding holding the breath and bearing down or locking at the end of either inhalation or exhalation, injury can be avoided. This is not the same process as locking the *bandha*, but the symptom of "fight or flight", of the parasympathetic nervous system. It is with the inhalation that the spine lengthens, particularly accentuating the tension around the three *granthi*, the three knots. The three *granthi* are linked to various illnesses. See the section on the *granthi* (page 27).

As a general rule strength (the inhalation) takes longer to develop than flexibility (the exhalation). As the two are inextricably linked, however, one cannot fully develop one without the other. Men tend to be more strong than flexible and women more flexible than strong. If these tendencies are exaggerated then imbalance occurs. The practice should balance these polarities. However, if there is a tendency to be more one way than the other, then the tendency should be accepted. It is useful to let the breathing be softer throughout the practice from time to time. Allow the breathing to dictate the practice rather than the other way around, doing all postures with less effort, working back from the ideal *āsana* rather than towards it. This allows greater ease in the practice, less heat is involved and it is less draining. Every breath, every posture, every sequence has its own particular ebb and flow. To resist this flow and try to control all of it is detrimental.

The state of health, general energy, mood, which sequence is being practiced, the cycle of the moon etc, are all influencing factors. Totally controlling the breath is basically impossible. One surrenders control *to* the breath, not the other way around. To let the breathing be completely passive and unconscious is also undesirable. Some practices will simply be more one way than the other. Eventually the two extremes of control/tension (inhalation) and relaxed/sloppy (exhalation) will become balanced.

Aṣṭāṅga Prāṇāyāma

Aṣṭāṅga prāṇāyāma is generally not taught until a student has at least completed Advanced A postures. That is, until the body has reached a point of stability with the *āsana, prāṇāyāma* is inadvisable. The *prāṇāyāma* practice taught in traditional *Aṣṭāṅga* differs from the more gentle practices usually taught. The long inhalation, exhalation and retention requires complete steadiness of body and mind: *sthira bhaga* or steady strength.

> When the whole system of *nāḍīs* which is full of impurities is cleaned, then the *yogi* becomes able to control the *prāṇa*...
>
> Just as lions, elephants and tigers are controlled by and by, so the breath is controlled by slow degrees, otherwise (i.e., by being hasty or using too much force) it kills the practitioner himself.
>
> *HYP,* 2: 5, 15

It is detrimental to learn *prāṇāyāma* from a book. If it is advisable to have a teacher to guide with *āsana* practice, with *prāṇāyāma* it is doubly so. Not only is the science of *prāṇāyāma* physically demanding, so too are its subtle effects. The ratios of breath retention to inhalation to exhalation and the numerological progression of this practice should be intimately understood. One does not cross the threshold of life and death lightly and one who rushes untimely toward this end does so at his or her own peril. What is achieved in life, the abilities that are accumulated, are never as important as realisation of what is. Focus on the process rather than the goal.

Once, when using the term *Śavāsana* in Guruji's presence I was told off. "Not *Śavāsana*! No. Corpse pose advanced practice. You take rest." The practice of "being dead" is a highly esoteric and dangerous process. It has been described earlier by Kriṣṇamacharya's ability to stop the heart beating. This may be a result of *prāṇāyāma* practice, but it is not the goal. In this light is *prāṇāyāma* viewed. Not until one is ready, which may be never in this life. Therefore, for the purpose of this book the finer details of *prāṇāyāma* practice have been omitted.

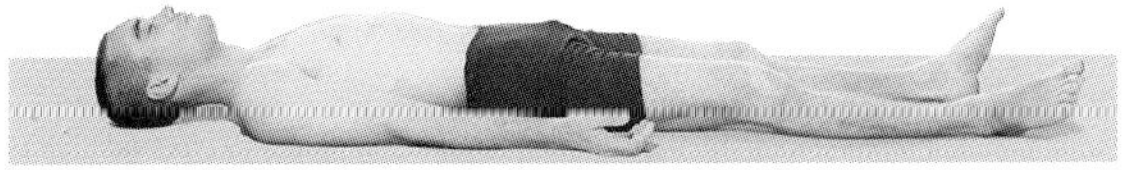

Take Rest!

Aṣṭāṅga Yogāsana

The *āsana* are the second component of the *tristhānaṁ,* or the body aspect. However, the traditional method of learning *Aṣṭāṅga yogāsana* begins with the mind as much as the body. When a complete beginner learns *Sūryanamaskara*, he or she repeats it until it is committed to memory, that is, body memory rather than just intellectual memory. Self-practice begins with the first class. It does not really matter how well (physically) the individual does it: there should be no judgement on how it looks. Memorising the practice is vital. This is often more confronting for a beginner than physically doing it.

After *Sūryanamaskara* and possibly one or two of the first standing postures the beginning student sits down, attempts some version of *Padmāsana* (sitting and breathing) and then lifts up in *Utpluthihiḥ*. Practice is finished in less than half an hour. Day by day, adding a maximum of one posture per day, a student learns the sequence. This is the traditional Mysore method. *Utpluthihiḥ* should always be done at the end of a practice, no matter how long or short the practice is. In particular the student should remember the essentials of what he or she has been taught before learning new postures.

This is not to say that this is the only way to teach *Aṣṭāṅga yoga*. It is common for many students to do led classes for the first few years as a way to become physically acclimatised. However, self practice is the most effective way for a student to remember. If beginning students are shown thirty postures in the sequence, they will only remember the first and the last posture (maybe). If they do just two postures at their own pace, they will remember them both. The slower it goes in, the deeper it penetrates.

Repetition is a key aspect of learning. As the postures are committed to memory there is a corresponding level of trust in the body: you know what you are doing, you know what comes next. There is no anxiety anticipating what the next thing will be. The physical aspect begins to develop with a gradual increase of flexibility and strength as the body and mind synchronise. It is most important to focus on the process rather than the outcome.

After a certain time practicing the Primary sequence, and if the ability is there, a student might begin learning the Intermediate postures. One by one these *āsana* are added to the Primary *āsana,* the total practice getting longer and longer. Eventually the student would practice only Intermediate. This is referred to as splitting the practice, that is, when a sequence is then practiced separately without adding those postures on to the previous sequence.

From one day to the next a student goes from regularly practicing all of Primary and at least half of Intermediate per session (usually over two hours) to just doing Intermediate (maybe one hour). The Primary sequence is then practiced once a week. Depending on the student, this can be a relief or a shock. The same process occurs when learning Advanced *āsana*. See the *vinyāsa* section (page 12) for more details.

The traditional method is relatively linear and methodical. Keep adding *āsana,* remembering the *vinyāsa* as you go, until you come to something you cannot do. You keep practicing up to the *āsana* that is difficult or impossible but you do not add new postures until you can do it effectively. This can be a little limiting but it does establish the body's capacity in the *āsana*. You become settled in the "seat". An unfortunate side-effect of this format is the tendency in *Aṣṭāṅga* to ask the question "What posture are you up to?" as if this indicates some kind of personal development. It is normal to want to move ahead, particularly as far as positive motivation and liveliness is concerned. The practice should never be lifeless, something new can be experienced every day, even if it is just a changed attitude. This forward looking attitude, however, should always be tempered with present tense awareness: stay in contact with what is rather than what should be.

Warming Up

Traditionally the very first action of practice is to stand in *Samasthitihiḥ,* chant the *mantra* and then continue with *Sūryanamskara A.* The body may not be warm and might feel particularly stiff. To launch into the first *Sūryanamaskara* without prior warm-ups may be daunting, particularly psychologically. This is often because of a desire to get it right first time, to look perfect. It is better to make it simpler, bend the knees, step back lightly etc, rather than injure oneself by doing flying jumps and full bends. This does not discount the validity of warming up, but credits the validity of not doing so. To begin without warming up is a matter of applying a relaxed state of awareness rather than a perfect state of body.

On the other hand, stretching before practice allows the body to wake up a little and renews awareness of any blind or weak spots. Of all the so called warm-ups that one may attempt, *uḍḍīyāna bandha* and *nauli kriyā* are considered the most traditional and practical (see page 16). If it helps to warm up, use whichever routine suits of the endless variations and feel free to experiment.

Alignment

Alignment is the ability to balance the various levels of the body and the mind into a working whole. Increasing your capacity to be straight in a posture should be encouraged, but there are limits to where the body can go. Alignment should never place undue pressure on the breath. If it does, this is the body's clear signal that there is too much pushing going on. If the breathing becomes truly unrestricted in a posture, then for that moment this is the best and most natural alignment possible, no matter how it looks.

It may take a great deal of learning, or unlearning, to stop pushing and encourage open behaviour. If there is a doubt or question as to what the correct alignment is, generally defer to the signals from your own body and breath even if it conflicts with external advice. It can be common, however, for a student's view of what is occurring to be different from what is actually occurring. A teacher is often necessary to point out this difference. To aid the development of awareness do not allow your breath to slide into complete apathy: attempt to be both active (inhalation) *and* relaxed (exhalation).

To force alignment on the body is a mistake. Your body's limit with an *āsana* is what it is, attempt to maximise your alignment from there. Accept how it is and be in your centre. The blind areas of mis-alignment, disease, discomfort and so on, will inevitably come to the surface and the body will heal what is possible to heal. Without continuous practice however, or consistency of awareness, the capacity to change is limited.

The belief that there is an anatomical or universal correct alignment is a judgement of right versus wrong. There are only *tendencies*. Every individual has a unique structure, the differing possibilities may be worlds apart. However, every individual needs some sense of alignment, or centredness in each posture to effectively develop awareness.

Balance the breath between aliveness and alignment in a posture and the tranquility of accepting it as it is. Be aware that the body usually has a very good reason for creating the so called mis-alignment or dis-ease in the first place. To try to force it back in to place is potentially more damaging than the original problem. Through acceptance change occurs, but only so far as is appropriate. Trust will develop as the body and mind begin to communicate more effectively and change will occur to the level that is needed. Do not seek to change: allow it to occur.

Core Postures

There are only three distinct *āsana* sequences in *Aṣṭāṅga yoga*. They are Primary, Intermediate and Advanced. However, as there are many more Advanced *āsana* than the others, the Advanced series has been organised into four sections, A, B, C and D. That is, six sequences in total. Each sequence starts with *Sūryanamaskara* and standing postures, though some of the final standing *āsana* are left aside when practicing the later sequences. Each has the same end: back bends and finishing postures. Each sequence has around thirty sitting postures.

The Primary sequence is called *yoga chikitsa*, meaning body therapy. There are two main areas which distinguish it from the other sequences: the emphasis on the hamstrings (forward bends) and the number of jumps. The repetitious nature of the sequence may become problematic. However, as the hamstring is a muscle, it tends to adapt and change more readily. If the hamstrings lengthen and the legs become stronger the lower back generally becomes more secure and supple. Conversely if the hamstring is over emphasised this will commonly destabilise the spine. Due patience should be observed in order not to push: focus on the process rather than the goal.

All forward bends contract the front of the body in some manner, purifying the internal organs. That is, body therapy. If the Primary sequence began with back bends, the overstimulation of the spine and nervous system would be premature: there would be many more complaints. The number of jumps in the Primary sequence can be problematic and initially exhausting. Some students tend to avoid the strength and jumping aspect of the Primary sequence by practising Intermediate prematurely. Overall strength and endurance is best developed in the Primary sequence.

In the Primary series there are a few core postures which are common stumbling blocks. They are *Marīchyāsana D, Kūrmāsana, Garbha Piṇḍāsana* and *Baddha Koṇāsana.* All of these postures can be quite confronting and some time and patience is usually necessary for the body to adapt. It is quite common for a student to practice (or be taught) the whole sequence prior to exploring these core *āsana* thoroughly. The final section of Primary is often more than a little messy as a result. Generally it is better to focus on these core postures first, rather than skimming over them to get to the finish line.

There are some basic requirements in these postures. For example, binding the hands in *Marīchyāsana D*. In this posture the front knee and both sit-bones may not go flat to the floor for some time, if at all. Binding the hands is the first crucial step. Being able to get the feet approximately behind the head in *Kurmāsana* is important. This posture may require an adjustment from the teacher most of the time. Many students, particularly

Figure 2.
Core Primary Postures.

Marīchyāsana D *Kūrmāsana* *Garbha Piṇḍāsana* *Baddha Koṇāsana*

those with shorter limbs, may not be able to bind the hands and keep the legs behind the head at the same time. Also of note is the previous posture to *Kurmāsana*: *Bhuja Pīḍāsana*. This posture requires a degree of strength which counterbalances the flexibility needed to get into *Kurmāsana*. There may be a tendency to be better at one than the other. That is, flexibility rather than strength or vice versa. Try to balance these *āsana* equally. Being able to get the knees flat in *Baddha Koṇāsana* is highly beneficial. If this posture improves then many of the previous postures such as *Garbha Piṇḍāsana* and *Marīchyāsana D* will become easier.

These four core *āsana*, also called binds, have a similar difficulty for many students. That is, immobility in the knees, hips and lower spine. Firstly, a consistent and gentle approach to practice will gradually help improve these areas. However, the following simple practice may also help:

Every evening do *Baddha Koṇāsana* with the spine upright against a wall. Do it while eating or reading and stay there for ten to twenty minutes. No other props are necessary. Also practice sitting in upright *Vīrāsana* (kneeling posture with the feet beside the hips and knees parallel). Do this posture with a blanket or pillow under the buttocks. Hold this for only five or ten minutes. Remember not to overdo it. Like any *āsana*, if practiced without care or without listening to the body it may cause some instability. Slowly the disposition of the knees and hips will improve.

The Intermediate sequence is called *nāḍī śodhana* meaning nervous system purification. This sequence begins with back bends, followed by their counterpart, legs-behind-the-head. The opposing nature of these postures creates a resonance in the nervous system. The second half of the sequence deals with both strength and more calming *āsana*. Intermediate can be over-stimulating at first. It is essential to get rest and decent sleep after practicing it. Strange dreams, heart palpitations and insomnia are common, often on top of bodily aches and pains.

Figure 3.
Core Intermediate Postures.

Pāśāsana *Kapotāsana* *Dwi Pāda Śīrṣāsana* *Karandavāsana*

The first requirement in the Intermediate core postures is being able to bind the hands in *Pāśāsana*. Getting the heels flat in this posture is also important though may not occur for some time. Binding the hands and balancing is the foundation. Binding the heels in *Kapotāsana* is considered a basic minimum, though merely touching the feet is a common starting point. Also of note is the previous posture to *Kapotāsana*: *Laghu Vajrāsana*. This *āsana* requires strength, counterbalancing the flexibility necessary to get into *Kapotāsana*. Similar to the pairing of *Bhuja Pīḍāsana* and *Kurmāsana*, each aspect of these *āsana* (strength and flexibility) needs to be balanced equally.

The difficulty in *Dwi Pāda Śīrṣāsana* can usually only be surmounted by regularly practicing the *āsana* itself. Or making a near attempt. For many students staying on this posture for some time (weeks or months or longer) is usually necessary. Getting down into *Karandavāsana* without assistance is a minimum standard. Coming up from this posture is not as likely or essential and may require more strength than is readily available. That is, coming up from this posture is not considered vital before moving on to the next posture.

The Advanced sequences (A, B, C and D) are called *sthira bhaga* meaning steady strength. They each require steadiness of body and mind. In particular, the practice of the arm balances in Advanced A requires a great deal of discipline to master. It is not the *āsana* that are necessarily difficult, it is the intensity of practicing them one after the other, the *vinyāsa*, that is often more challenging. A fellow teacher adequately summed up the effects of practicing Advanced with the following words: "It knocks the stuffing out of you!" Nevertheless, strength is developed. Core postures for the Advanced sequences are not specified as they are too individual: every posture is core!

A minimum ability with the core *āsana* is assumed before the student is usually allowed to move on to the next posture. Ideally one should be able to complete every *āsana* without any assistance. It is common for a student to be held at the core *āsana* a lot longer than the others in the sequence. However, it is not essential to do these *āsana* perfectly before moving on: just do not avoid them, find out what the body's limits are first! The postures become progressively more difficult with each sequence. In the Primary sequence the ability to do the *āsana* well is important but some allowance for individual capacity and expression is encouraged. In Intermediate there is less leeway and the postures need to be done with a minimum amount of fluidity, particularly for safety's sake. In Advanced there is almost no leeway.

With all core postures (or any posture that is difficult) it can be useful to repeat the posture two or three times in the same practice. Avoid over-straining and stop if the breathing becomes too restricted. Each time it is done there will be a change in awareness, a slightly different way of doing it. The body adapts and the posture improves. Repetition does not entertain, it teaches. Keep in mind, however, that repeating a posture in the same practice is disruptive and may detract from other vital qualities. Ideally the practice is a consistent flow, the body moves with the breath and the mind follows.

The concept of core *āsana* is not a traditional understanding of the practice. As there are always exceptions to the rule as far as ability is concerned, the idea that any one posture is more difficult than any other is completely relative to the individual. As a generalisation, however, it holds true: the *āsana* mentioned here are commonly the most difficult. It is important not to practice the sequence and leave them out, in the too hard basket.

Jump Throughs and Jump Backs

When learning jump throughs and jump backs, try to optimise both the feeling of lightness (no strain) and strength, particularly in the mid-section. One without the other is an imbalance. It is not necessary or desirable to push to achieve the complete floating action: for some this may never happen. It is applying the right attitude with the right technique which achieves optimum strength and lightness.

Jumping into and out of the postures should be standardised. Jump through with the legs crossed rather than straight legged. Lead with the knees, not with the feet and the centre of your body will tend to engage. The straight legged jump through should only be practiced if you can jump through cross legged: to float back and float through with control and *without* touching the feet to the floor (Figure 5). The straight legged jump through is easier for some students and does not develop strength as effectively.

When learning, keep the feet back and allow them to land on the floor first before coming through. This may be the first few years of practice! Also do the same when jumping back: place the hands in front of the feet rather than behind them (Figure 4). Try to slow down the jump through at this half-way point (just between the arms) rather than trying to hurry the feet through with little or no control. When jumping through, keep the feet back and the toes pointed when you land. Avoid flexing them at all unless you can hold the lift in mid-air. Try to keep the hips up and use the breath (inhalation) to help.

Figure 4.
Jump into and out of the cross-legged position (slowly!)

Keep the hips up and the knees off the floor.
Bring the knees through first! The feet come through last (if at all).

Keep the toes pointed and land on the little-toe edge of the foot rather than the ball of the foot. Also, keep the hands flat.

Do not attempt to jump directly into a sitting posture without making the transition through *lolāsana*. (Figure 4 or figure 5.) To develop strength effectively *always* jump through and jump back with legs crossed. Some postures such as *Bhuja Pīḍāsana* and *Kūrmāsana* are obvious exceptions. When jumping back from both sides of a posture it is useful to alternate crossing the legs on each side. Jump through and jump back on the right side of the posture with the right leg underneath and jump through and jump back on the left side of the posture with the left leg underneath.

Figure 5.

"Floating" through (into *Navāsana*) and "floating" back.

Core Strength

A common perception of many practitioners, particularly women, is a lack of core strength. That is, little or no progress with float backs. As the practice does require strength to maintain, there is some validity to this view. However, do not focus too much on core/*mūla bandha* strength at the expense of other areas of the practice (such as overall strength) or they may suffer. Usually if there is no core strength *also* there is no overall strength. In general the abdominal and lower back region should be strengthened and supported throughout the practice. Do the practice with consistent awareness of any weaknesses and the body will usually assert its own organic sense of balance.

Core strength is ideal for everyone, but particularly useful for lower back difficulty, or when there is over development in the upper body. Because of the emphasis on the jumps in the sequence upper body strength is also emphasised, at least initially. Arm strength is important and to ignore this in favour of core strength may be detrimental. Both are useful. By using the arms effectively you can begin to access the lateral muscles of the torso and then the "core" of the abdominal region. That is, throughout the practice keep the shoulder blades sliding down the back rather than rising up to the ears. This decreases tension in the upper shoulder and trapezius muscles and is particularly useful when doing the jumps and the *chaturaṅga*/up dog/down dog *vinyāsa*. With the shoulders down and elbows generally tucked in, both the latisimus dorsi and intercostal muscles will begin to engage. In time, any aggravation in the neck and shoulders will disperse as the overall practice improves.

Unlike most other *yoga* methods *Aṣṭāṅga yoga* develops strength as much as flexibility. This is largely due to consistency and repetition of practice. If strength is over developed in areas where it already exists or remains underdeveloped in blind areas, seek to re-balance this. Ideally you should be able hold the weight of the whole body from any other part of the body: balance on one foot, on the back, belly, head, hands etc. In this way each part of the body is strong *relative* to the next. The interconnectedness of the body should become apparent. From this point of view it does not matter if you can "float back" (and hold *mūla bandha*) or not. Your body will become more balanced, relative for you.

The concept of core strength is intertwined with that of core stability. One without the other is impossible. To push too much to achieve the desired core strength will ultimately destabilise the body. The spine is another aspect of the core, particularly the relationship between the movements of the spine and the various abdominal muscles. This can be a complex area to examine. As the breath becomes longer and softer, the spine can reach its maximum potential with all range of movements. As with trying to control the breath, trying to control the spine and abdomen at all times is undesirable. The spine is always moving. To hold it rigidly decreases the spine's ability to articulate. As the ability and awareness in a posture increases, the sense of the subtle movements of the spine and abdomen should also increase. Pay particular attention to the movement of breath as it affects the different regions of the spine and the core will begin to stabilise.

There are many techniques to aid the development of core strength or strength in any part of the body for that matter. Often it does take an external point of view to bring attention to the blind or dead areas of the practice. If a particular technique increases awareness in a blind area, then use it. Just remember that it is awareness alone that is the key.

Back Bends and Handstand

The first back bending posture in the sequence is *Ūrdhva Mukha Svanāsana*, or upward dog. In upward dog there is a tendency to move the head too quickly and the neck and diaphragm often lock up as a result. This can have an adverse effect on the lower back. Try to move the head back at the very last when arching in this posture. Also give most importance to the breath (the inhalation) rather than over arching, or forcing correct alignment. i.e. inhale completely without any locking or bearing down of the ribs and diaphragm. The breath may pause at the end, but it is not tight or held. It can be useful to hold this posture for longer than a single inhalation (for two or three breaths instead) particularly after *Navāsana* and *Kurmāsana* when it may be more difficult to arch. This posture counterbalances all of the forward bends and the contracted nature of the jumps.

Figure 6.
Half-bending.

The traditional Mysore method of back bending is to restrict all students to Primary *āsana* until they can drop back into *Ūrdhva Dhanurāsana* (and come up) on their own. That is, no Intermediate *āsana* until you can do drop backs, even if the initial Intermediate back bends are easier. Some leeway can be given with this rule, but practicing the drop back should not be ignored. It takes energy and perseverance. If it is difficult to complete the full drop back to the floor, half-bending (figure 6) can be practiced regularly. Arch the back from an upright standing position with the arms crossed over the chest. Bend back on the exhalation and move down towards the floor a little way and then back up again on the inhalation: one breath with one movement repeated a few times. Gradually develop the strength and control in the legs and spine, and only add the arm movement (to the floor) if there is little or no pain.

The photographic section of this book shows the most common order of transition from (1) drop backs, to (2) handstand drop-overs, to (3) full *Viparīta Chakrāsana*, rather than the traditional variation of doing (3) *Viparīta Chakrāsana* before (2) handstand drop-overs. (See page 48). An important aspect of the back bend/handstand sequence, particularly the order of it, is that handstands *are not* a part of the Primary sequence. Until the Primary *āsana* are developed sufficiently and Intermediate is begun, handstands should be left aside. Develop the jump backs, drop backs and headstand well before attempting this advanced *āsana*. Increase the strength of the arms and abdomen (jump backs) the flexibility of the spine (drop backs) and the ability to balance (headstand) to gain the proper ability with the handstand.

The correct order of learning the inverted postures is: first shoulder-stand, then headstand, then the fore-arm balance (*Pincha Mayūrāsana*) and then handstand. This means that a student would not normally begin handstand until he or she has completed *Pincha Mayūrāsana* in the Intermediate sequence. However, as handstand is a part of the back bending sequence, it is useful to commence its regular practice at the same time the student commences Intermediate. The student's ability with headstand (balance) and with flexibility and strength (drop backs and jump backs) will determine the degree to which handstand will improve. There are some *āsana* that most people want to be able to practice straight away: the lotus posture, drop backs, splits and handstands. Each of these should be learnt in its own time. All of the foundation work done in the Primary and Intermediate sequences will lead to these *āsana*.

Variations in the Sequence

The variation of doing *Trivikramāsana* and *Supta Trivikramāsana* (standing and lying splits) after *Utthita Hasta Pādāṅguṣṭhāsana* and *Supta Pādāṅguṣṭhāsana* respectively has been left out of the main section of this book since they are not Primary *āsana*. However, they are an accepted part of the practice. In general one should have completed all of Primary before commencing to practice these Advanced *āsana*. If one of these is practiced (e.g. *Trivikramāsana*) you should do both (*Supta Trivikramāsana*). Also it is best to do these *āsana* after completing both sides of *Pādāṅguṣṭhāsana* (whether standing or lying) rather than doing it in the middle between sides. (Figure 7). This keeps each *āsana* separate and clear and allows a short rest between them.

Figure 7.

Utthita Hasta Pādāṅguṣṭhāsana (left side) ☞ *Trivikramāsana* (right and left)

In times past *Hanumānāsana* and *Sama Koṇāsana* (front and side splits) were sometimes practiced after *Prasārita Pādottānāsana D* (sometimes including handstands). This practice is no longer a part of the accepted form. One problem is not being sufficiently warm and open to practice these at the start. Most importantly, however, Primary and Intermediate *āsana* should be attended to before rushing into Advanced *āsana*. Also, both splits postures are sitting *āsana* and to go to the floor in the middle of a standing sequence unnecessarily interrupts the flow and energy of the upright postures. The splits postures are practiced near the end of their respective sequences when the body is more open.

It is standard for most *vinyāsa* to do the right side first: step to the right, move the right leg, fold it in position etc. *Pāśāsana* is one exception to this rule. It is traditional to sit in *Padmāsana* with the right foot folded first. The right heel (lower) accentuates the descending colon and spleen. The left heel (higher) accentuates the ascending colon and liver. This is considered the correct crossing energetically; male (right) and female (left), particularly for meditation. However, after the first year or so of practice, it is useful to begin crossing the legs in *Padmāsana* on the alternate side in order to balance the knees and hips. This is also true for *Kūrmāsana, Dwi Pāda Śīrṣāsana* and *Yoga Nidrāsana.*

Another variation is the inclusion of the twisted *Pārśvakoṇāsana* in the sequence. As this posture is considered to be an Intermediate *āsana*, traditionally it is not taught to beginners. Lastly, the practice of *jñāna mudrā* (thumb and fore-finger together) should only be maintained while sitting in the final *Padmāsana* and in *Mūla Bandhāsana* and *Yoga Daṇḍāsana*. The thumb represents universal consciousness (*Brahman*) and the fore-finger represents individual consciousness (*ātman*) yoked together as one. In all other postures the *mudrā* should be left aside as it is energetically stimulating and a distraction from doing the posture in its simplicity.

The Nine *Dṛiṣṭi*

Dṛiṣṭi is often defined as "looking place" but literally means "perception". By keeping the gaze to the traditional *dṛiṣṭi*, *pratyāhāra* or withdrawal of the mind from external judgement is cultivated. Eventually a new perception takes place. As the third component of the *tristhānaṁ*, the mind aspect, the *dṛiṣṭi* are sometimes considered less important and left aside for too long. Stay in contact with the here and now of bodily awareness, rather than constantly looking (and judging) on the outside. The tendency to look around at other individuals practicing nearby should be avoided. Keep your consciousness within the field of your body and this inner awareness will unfold.

The *dṛiṣṭi* written in the photographic section of this book may vary a little from current standards. As Guruji has previously written, the *dṛiṣṭi* follow a definite pattern, linked with the breath and the *vinyāsa*. Odd numbered *vinyāsa*, or inhalations, are linked with upward movements and the gaze moves up to the third eye. This *dṛiṣṭi* emphasises openness in the heart area. Even numbered *vinyāsa*, or exhalations, are linked with downward movements and the gaze moves down to the tip of the nose. The *nasagrai dṛiṣṭi* emphasises the root *mūla bandha* and is the most common gazing point. (See *Sūryanamaskara A & B*, page 36).

An exception to this is upward dog and most backbends. With these postures the *dṛiṣṭi* can either be the tip of the nose or the third eye. Looking up and back (anything overhead, including the third eye) has an expansive effect on the body and consciousness. This can tend to aggravate the body in areas where it may be weak. Looking down at the body (particularly the nose or navel) tends to keep attention inward and the body stable. In downward dog the standard *dṛiṣṭi* is the navel. If this gaze tends to hunch the spine, gazing at the nose-tip is a suitable alternative. Similarly with all forward bends: if the foot *dṛiṣṭi* tends to over arch the neck, then the nose *dṛiṣṭi* is more suitable. If looking at the nose is difficult, then maintaining the gaze in that same direction is enough. Do not become cross-eyed. Each of the gazes aids concentration and awareness; practice them with diligence and patience.

Figure 8.

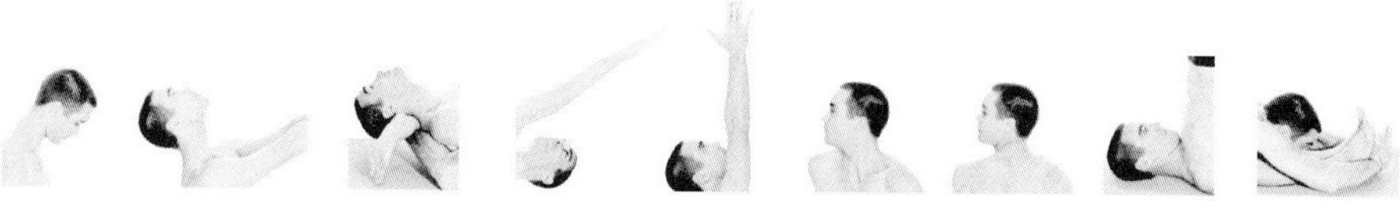

1 2 3 4 5 6 7 8 9

The nine traditional gazing places (figure 8 - *nawa dṛiṣṭi*) are as follows:
1) Nose or *nasagrai dṛiṣṭi*, 2) Upwards or *ūrdhva dṛiṣṭi*, 3) Third eye or *ājñā chakra dṛiṣṭi*, 4) Hand or *hastagrai dṛiṣṭi*, 5) Thumbs or *aṅguṣṭha madyai dṛiṣṭi*, 6) Right side or *pārśva dṛiṣṭi*, 7) Left side or *pārśva dṛiṣṭi*, 8) Navel or *nabi dṛiṣṭi* and 9) Foot or *pādayoragrai dṛiṣṭi*.

In between the *āsana* it is not advised to keep strict *dṛiṣṭi*, but neither should one look around, for example, between *trikoṇāsana* and coming back to *samasthitiḥ*. In such cases keep the eyes generally lowered and the focus internal. Lastly, avoid wearing glasses or contact lenses while you practice and the *dṛiṣṭi* will help improve your eyesight.

Aṣṭāṅga Vinyāsa

Vinyāsa literally (and only) means movement. There are the external movements of the body and the internal movements of breath and when linking these movements together (inhale up, exhale down etc.) the movements of consciousness may be harnessed. This facilitates the upward movement of the three *bandha*. Movement is a universal aspect of nature and occurs on many levels simultaneously.

> O *Yogi*, do not do *āsana* without *vinyāsa* - Ṛiṣi Vamana.

> Esoterically movement is the most primal act of existence. Without this simple thing, there would be no universe, no us, no experience, nothing. Light is movement... God is movement. Also dance alone is the only creative act in which there is a perfect oneness of the creator and his creation. Unlike a painting, a poem, an invention or any other artistic impulse, when the dance is over there is no product, no thing to save and enjoy. As with life, we may perceive the dance, never possess it. One cannot separate the dancer from dancing, just as one cannot separate God from the world or from ourselves. Of special meaning is the place where *Śiva* dances: in the *chitsabhā*, the hall of consciousness. In other words it [the divine play of God] happens within each of us.
>
> *Dancing with Śiva, xix.*

The *vinyāsa* in the traditional *Aṣṭāṅga* practice are variations on the theme of *Sūryanamaskara*. It is from this foundation that all other movements flow. The Salute to the Sun begins in *Samasthitiḥ*, meaning equal upright. The practice of full *vinyāsa* means to come back to this equilibrium from each posture (or after the second side of a posture that has left and right) whether standing, sitting, lying or inverted. (Figure 9). The equilibrium of *Samasthitiḥ* implies both physical and mental balance. The practice of half *vinyāsa* is to come back to downward dog between (sitting) postures. i.e. half of *Sūryanamaskara*. (Figure 10).

The cycle of full *vinyāsa* begins and ends with *Samasthitiḥ*, or jumping up to standing between sitting postures (Figure 9), though only to downward dog between sides of the same posture. The practice of half *vinyāsa* is to jump back to downward dog between all sitting postures (Figure 10). Unless otherwise indicated one should jump back from most postures in the latter fashion. Initially, when learning the Primary sequence one can elect not to jump back between sides of the same posture but to simply change over (Figure 11).

When adding on postures from one sequence to another the learning *vinyāsa* is also appropriate (fewer jumps to conserve energy.) The level of experience and well being of the student should dictate whether full *vinyāsa* is suitable. It is a common view that the practice of full *vinyāsa* develops greater strength. To an extent this may be true, however, it can be laborious and one may lose energy and concentration as a result. It is consistency and constant attention that increases true strength and endurance. Doing a shorter practice and doing it well (with greater awareness) is far more beneficial than doing a longer practice badly (with an over-achieving mind-set.)

Figure 9.
Full *vinyāsa* from downward dog (i.e. from a sitting posture.)
Note: the hands do not come overhead just prior to *Samasthitiḥ*.

Figure 10.
Half *vinyāsa*

Figure 11.
Learning *vinyāsa*

Please note, many of the *vinyāsa* portrayed in this introduction are examples and may be incomplete in some way. Consult the *vinyāsa* section of this book for the most standard and complete form.

Vinyāsa Krama

Vinyāsa krama is the "moving by numbers" method of teaching rather than self practice. That is, a led or guided class where the students move together at pace with the teacher's count. *Krama* means one by one. Inhalations are linked with odd numbered *vinyāsa*, (1, 3, 5 etc.) and exhalations are linked with even numbered *vinyāsa* (2, 4, 6 etc.) (See page 36, Salute to the Sun). When trying to follow the Sanskrit counting used in this method it may be initially confusing. Typically all of the essential *vinyāsa* are counted using Sanskrit, *ekam, dve, trini,* but all of the breaths within a posture are counted in English (one, two, three etc.)

Also the Sanskrit counting omits certain numbers. For example, when moving through a posture and jumping back, the teacher (typically Guruji or Sharath) may have spoken through the numbers 19 and 20 (*ekunavimsatiḥ* and *vimsatiḥ*) after jumping back, but all of a sudden he is back at number 7 (*sapta*). (See figure 12) This is simply because the instructor has physically cut out the full *vinyāsa*, jumping up to *Samasthitiḥ*, but started again with the numbers as if you had done it: from downward dog into the next posture. To keep it consistent, the teacher simply starts counting for half *vinyāsa* at number 7 each time you jump through to a new posture. Some numbers also seem to be more auspicious, hence the inexplicable gaps of counting between some *vinyāsa*.

Figure 12.

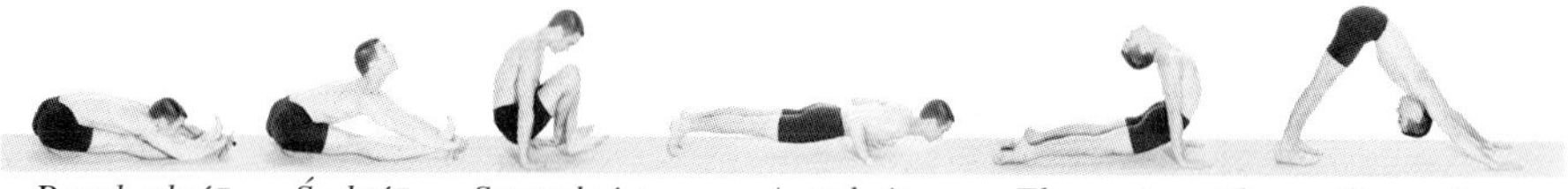

Panchadaśā 15 — *Śodaśā* 16 — *Saptadaśā* 17 — *Aṣṭādaśā* 18 — *Ekunavimsatiḥ* 19 — *Vimsatiḥ...* 20

...Vimsatiḥ/Śat 20/6 — *Sapta* 7 — *Aṣṭau* 8 — *Nawa* 9 — *Daśā* 10 — *Ekādaśā* 11 etc.

All *vinyāsa krama* counting is based on full *vinyāsa,* whether you have come back to standing or not. This includes some of the standing postures, particularly the often tricky *vinyāsa* of *Pādottānāsana* A, B, C & D. If these four postures are practiced coming back to *Samasthitiḥ* after each, the *vinyasās* (counting to 5 each time) are consistent. In any case the movements for these postures should be memorised: the *vinyāsa* for *Pādottānāsana A* and *D* is the same and for *B* and *C* is the same.

Figure 13.

Panchadaśā 15 — *Śodaśā* 16 — *Saptadaśā* 17 — *Aṣṭādaśā* 18 — *Ekunavimsatiḥ* 19 — *Vimsatiḥ* 20

Ekā-vimsatiḥ 21 — *Dvā-vimsatiḥ* 22 — (0) — *Ekam* 1 — *Dve* 2 — *Trini* 3 — *Chatuari* 4 — *Pancha* 5 — *Śat* 6

Figure 13 shows the full *vinyāsa* out of *Jānu Śīrṣāsana B*. The counting method is based on the *vinyāsa*, either a posture or a particular movement, not the breath. So whether one holds a posture for half a breath, one breath or twenty, it has only one number (*one vinyāsa*) allocated to it. The numbers for the *vinyāsa* indicated in this book (see pages 50 - 79) although accurate, may deviate in some cases from the current standard. Some details have changed over the years and will inevitably change again in the future. The counting method is also clearly detailed in Lino Miele's *Ashtanga Yoga, Series I & II*.

Vinyāsa after Splitting

When learning the Intermediate series the standard process is to do the full Primary sequence up to *Setu Bandhāsana* and then add on the Intermediate *āsana* one by one. The adding on process continues until at least *Eka Pāda Śīrṣāsana,* though sometimes until *Karandavāsana* or longer. From then on the student practices Intermediate alone up to *Karandavāsana* (for example) with the remaining *āsana* of that sequence added day by day. Primary is then practiced on its own once a week, typically on Friday. This is referred to as splitting the practice. The same process of splitting applies when adding Advanced A *āsana* to Intermediate, or adding Advanced B to Advanced A: splitting the sequence at approximately *Viranchyāsana B* for Advanced A and *Puṅga Kukkuṭāsana* for Advanced B. That is, you should add more than half of each sequence before you practice it separately.

When practicing Intermediate or Advanced *āsana* on their own, the traditional practice is to stop doing standing postures after *Pārśvottānāsana* and to commence the *vinyāsa* for that series from there. However, it is advisable to keep practicing the two balance poses that follow it, particularly *Utthita Hasta Pādāṅguṣṭhāsana* (Figure 7). As this *āsana* is found to be difficult for many students, it is useful to practice it every day. Also, the first full *vinyāsa* for Primary begins with *Utkaṭāsana*. That is, *Utkaṭāsana* is in fact the first Primary posture, not *Daṇḍāsana*. As the *vinyāsa* for *Pāśāsana* is almost exactly the same, the Intermediate sequence can be begun the same way as *Utkaṭāsana* (Figure 14).

Figure 14.

From *Ardha Baddha Padmottānāsana* into *Pāśāsana*.
Recommended *vinyāsa* into Intermediate (and Advanced) *āsana* after being split.

When adding Advanced A postures to Intermediate one leaves off the final headstand postures and commences with *Vasiṣṭhāsana* after *Supta Ūrdhva Pāda Vajrāsana* (Figure 15). The Advanced sequences are sometimes practiced without doing any standing postures. One commences the first Advanced posture (*Vasiṣṭhāsana* or *Mūla Bandhāsana*) after *Sūryanamaskara B*. This has some benefits, such as a shorter and sharper practice, though the body is less open to begin with. All of the sequences should be completed with back bending, inverted *āsana* and the final sitting postures, or as much of these as you can manage.

Figure 15.

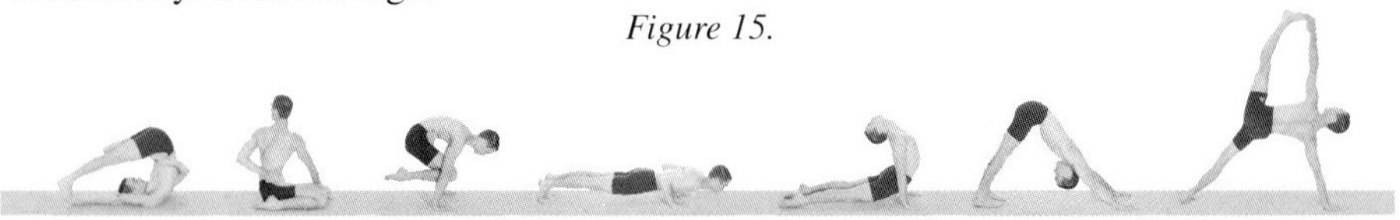

From *Supta Ūrdhva Pāda Vajrāsana* into *Vasiṣṭhāsana*.

The Three *Bandha*

Bandha is defined as "binding, tying a bond, tie, chain, fetter, a ligature, to catch, hold captive, arrest, imprison, fix, fasten, hold back, restrain, stop, shut close, to redirect, clot and lock." The basic premise of the *bandha* is that by restraining or locking the muscles on a physical level, a subtle unlocking occurs on a mental or energetic level. With most *āsana* practice one locks and unlocks various muscle groups in turn. By the end of a practice, particularly when taking rest, the body and mind can completely unwind, bringing a heightened sense of relaxation and awareness. This is one aspect of the paradox of the *bandha*. When you completely let go, then the *bandha* become naturally active.

There are three principal *bandha*. They are *mūla bandha*, *jālandhara bandha* and *uḍḍīyāna bandha*. *Mūla* means root, *jālandhara* means net in the stream, and *uḍḍīyāna* means to fly upwards. The *mūla bandha* is the most subtle, the *jālandhara* both physical and subtle and the *uḍḍīyāna* the most gross of the three. They are also known as the "three throats" through which vital forces pass: the throat, the diaphragm and the anus. The *mūla bandha* locks and seals energy from the lower end of the body, minimising physical depletion. The upper *jālandhara bandha* locks and seals energy from the upper end, minimising mental agitation. The *uḍḍīyāna bandha* applies pressure from within, increasing the internal fire or *agni*, improving both the physical and energetic digestive system. When all three are maintained simultaneously it is known as the *mahā bandha* or great lock.

Mūla Bandha

The breath, movement (*vinyāsa*) and *bandha* are all inextricably linked. The *mūla bandha* is subtly activated with every breath. That is, the inhalation involves an increase in *prāṇa* and a corresponding increase in energy originating at the pelvic floor. However, when you are unaware of your breath, the *bandha* movement is slight. When the breathing becomes more conscious, so too the *bandha*. With the exhalation, because of the contraction involved, it is usually easier to feel a physical restriction at the *mūla bandha* area (pelvic floor/perineum), particularly when the out-breath is extended. Deep breathing facilitates an upward movement of *prāṇa*, or an increase in energy and awareness.

> Pressing *yoni* (perineum)...contract up the anus. By drawing the *apāna* (downward energy) thus, *mūla bandha* is made.
>
> *HYP*, 2: 60

> Pressing well the anus (perineum) with the heel, draw upwards the *apāna vāyu* slowly by practice. This is described as the *mūla bandha* - the destroyer of decay and death. If, in the course of the practice of this *mudrā* the *yogi* can unite the *apāna* with the *prāṇa vāyu*, then it becomes of course the *yoni-mudrā* (female seal). He who has accomplished the *yoni-mudrā*, what can he not accomplish in this world? Sitting in the *Padmāsana*, free from idleness, the *yogi*, leaving the ground, moves through the air by virtue of this *mudrā*.
>
> *Śiva Samhita*, 4: 41, 42, 44

The following breathing exercise is helpful in feeling the physical link to the *mūla bandha* (figure 16). The body moves in a wavelike pattern with the expansion of the breath. This wave motion mirrors the wavelike structure of the spine. As the breath is extended, at the crest of the wave, the *mūla bandha* is also at its peak. Begin by sitting upright in any comfortable position. Exhale fully. Begin inhaling slowly. (1) The start of the inhalation expands the belly, (2) the middle section expands the ribs and chest to the collarbone/sternum area, (3) the last portion of the inhalation contracts the lower belly. This last movement may be slight.

Figure 16.

(1) Belly expands (2) Chest expands (3) Belly contracts

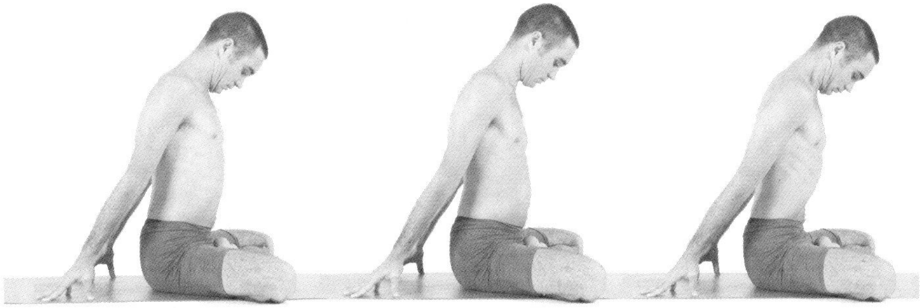

(1) Belly releases (2) Chest deflates (3) Belly contracts

In reverse, as the breath is released, (1) the lower belly starts to come out as the lower contraction is released, (2) next the chest and ribs deflate, contracting inwards, (3) finally the lower belly comes in again. The last lower contraction may be slight. In general allow this process to occur and feel the *mūla bandha* as you stretch the breath: do not arbitrarily impose what you think should happen. The lower belly only does the final contracted movement at the end of inhalation and exhalation when the breathing is lengthened close to its maximum capacity. Repeat the exercise and pay particular attention to the perineum/*mūla bandha* area. If the breath is extended to its maximum (inhalation or exhalation) the *mūla* tension increases. One can then feel some type of *mūla* contraction occurring naturally. It is useful to note that the quality of the *mūla* contraction at the end of the inhalation is different to that at the end of the exhalation.

Note: the exercise above is an example to aid awareness only. It is not intended for regular practice as it can also inhibit the natural process. Also, this breathing process may differ to other *yogic* breathing that is taught. Personally, I believe that you should allow your breath to be as organic as possible. It is unnecessary and generally inadvisable to hold the lower belly clenched throughout the practice. Whatever allows the most freedom of movement without causing undue discomfort or instability is best.

In the case of injury, lower back difficulty, particular stiffness or weakness, it is therapeutic to maintain contact with *mūla bandha*. That is, keep the lower belly/pelvic floor firm throughout the practice, rather than being completely unaware of it. Also when attempting a difficult *āsana*, keeping the *mūla bandha* area engaged can also be useful, e.g. jump backs or a particularly deep back bend. However, exaggerating this *bandha* will tend to over develop the physical contraction. Allow some movement rather than trying to hold this area immobilised or in later years there may be some trouble in reversing a repetitive strain injury.

To habitually contract the perineum or sphincter can also block the *mūla bandha* from arising at all. Not only are there psychological tensions associated with this habit, the physical tension tends to overly contract many of the other muscles in the pelvic floor region, inhibiting their ability to relax. For it is only in a fully relaxed state the true *mūla bandha* begins to arise. To arrive at this relaxed state, free from tension, usually requires the steady application of contraction *and* release throughout the practice. Most upward movements are linked with inhalations and are associated with strength. Most downward movements are linked with exhalations and are associated with flexibility. This is the *vinyāsa* system. Simply put, the practice of developing the breathing and *vinyāsa* will accentuate the movements of the *bandha* without having to habitually make them occur.

Focusing the breath is a little like stretching a rubber band. As one end of the rubber band is stretched away from a bound point, the bound point is inevitably pulled up in order to make balance (rising *mūla* tension). As the inhalation progresses (up), the diaphragm lowers. The more the diaphragm drops (lengthening the lower spine) the more it begins to accentuate the *mūla* contraction. The inhalation is both an upward *and* a downward movement. As the exhalation progresses (down), the diaphragm lifts. The more the diaphragm lifts (accentuating the classic *uḍḍīyāna bandha*) the more it begins to accentuate the rising *mūla* tension. The exhalation is both a downward *and* an upward movement. Each inhalation and each exhalation are both an *apānic* and *prāṇic* process (downward and upward energy). One aspect is simply more gross/physical, the other aspect more subtle/energetic. They are mirrors of each other and eventually they unite. It should be noted that for some students the diaphragm may be held or may move in patterns other than that described above. As the practice evolves and awareness changes then the processes described generally become the norm.

The *mūla bandha* can be felt on both the inhalation and the exhalation. In both cases the energetic movement is up the spine, transforming the normal, downward *apānic* movement. Understanding the *mūla bandha* can be difficult. Generally, allow it to occur through means of the breath rather than forcing a physical habit. That is, whatever you think *mūla bandha* to be, that's probably not it. Do not seek to do it, allow it to occur. For more details on this subject refer to the three *granthi* (page 27).

The location of the *mūlādhāra chakra* is different for men and women. For women it is higher: at the cervix. For men it is closer to the surface: above the perineum and below the prostate. (See figure 17.) When trying to isolate the *mūla* contraction, the following exercise may help. Lie on the back with the knees bent up and the feet flat to the floor. Touch the perineum with the middle finger of one hand. Start conscious breathing (inhalation or exhalation) and contract first the muscles of the belly and then the muscles of the buttocks alternatively. When the belly is contracted, relax the buttocks. When the buttocks are contracted, relax the belly. This is not as easy as it first may seem. The perineal muscle should also contract, particularly as one increases both the length of breath and the front and back contractions. For women, try to feel this contraction as cervical rather than perineal. Next try to relax both the belly and buttocks and contract the perineum/cervix *only*. This isolation is more difficult and may take some time to master.

Figure 17.
Note: The arrow indicating the *mūlādhāra chakra* travels through the perineum.

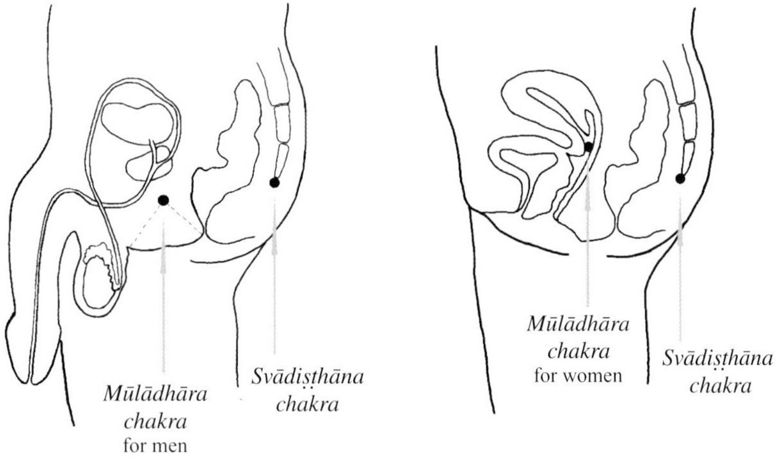

In the general practice it is enough to bring your attention to the perineal area. As you extend the breath the awareness of the *mūla* area should increase. From this perspective it is not at all necessary or desirable to apply *mūla bandha* at all. The *āsana* practice is often difficult enough without trying to impose extra techniques. Increase awareness rather than increasing imposition and pressure. The process of extending the breath and feeling the *mūla bandha* is flowing and does not unduly interfere with the natural balance, flexibility and strength inherent in each posture. To explore these processes thoroughly takes time and commitment. Focus primarily on the breath. As the breath is constantly moving, it is difficult to get stuck with it. Allow the *bandha* (and *dṛiṣṭi*) to evolve through breathing awareness. For it is more than likely that the *bandha* will take many years to develop. As a fellow teacher once said, "If you find *mūla bandha* let me know where it is!"

One area to specifically focus the *mūla bandha* is in *Utpluthiḥ*. This is the very last action of every sequence. It can be pivotal for accessing untapped energy, especially as there is the tendency to be most tired when attempting to "uproot". The breathing should be both slow and deliberate, particularly the inhalation, accentuating the rising *prāṇa*.

Jālandhara Bandha

> Contract the throat and press the chin firmly down towards the chest. This is called *jālandhara bandha*, which destroys old age and death.
>
> *SS*, 2: 69

The *jālandhara bandha* can be emphasised in *Padmāsana*, or almost any upright sitting posture for *prāṇāyāma* purposes. It is best to have some experience of it before attempting *uḍḍīyāna bandha*. *Jāla* means net and *andhara* means stream. Like a net, this *bandha* is meant to catch *amṛita*, or heavenly elixir, and stop it from escaping downwards into the body. This is symbolic for directing consciousness towards higher principles, controlling both thought and speech, and not allowing negative thoughts to poison the body.

Sit in *Padmāsana* (or any comfortable sitting posture) with the hands on the knees in *jñāna mudrā*. Tuck the chin in slightly, keep the back of the neck long without collapsing and the heart area lifted. Breathe in fully. At the end of the inhalation, lower the chin slightly, gently engage *mūla bandha*, then apply the chin lock. The area around the middle of the throat (Adams apple for men) is both contracted and drawn downwards slightly. The chin should be as close to the chest as possible, though for some it does not touch. Hold for three to four seconds. Release the chin a little first and then breathe out softly. This is called *antara kumbhaka,* or internal retention. Minimise the head movement when applying this *bandha*. That is, lift the head slightly when releasing the lock, and lower it slightly when applying it. Allow the chest to move as fully as possible, particularly with the inhalation. Retention on the exhalation (with or without *uḍḍīyāna bandha*) takes more practice and perseverance. This is called *bāhya kumbhaka* or external retention. There can be a tendency to either over resist or panic with the latter retention, so the body should be both stable and strong.

In the *vinyāsa* practice the breath should never be held or stopped completely. By simply maintaining *ujjāyi* breathing there is a natural control and restraint of the breath: the most general form of *jālandhara bandha*. This *bandha* is described here not to examine *kumbhaka* but as an aid to understanding the general practice. The ability to inhale for at least thirty seconds should be achieved before exploring the more intense *prāṇāyāma* practices.

Uḍḍīyāna Bandha

> The *uḍḍīyāna bandha*: the belly above the navel is pressed backwards towards the spine. The *uḍḍīyāna* is like a lion for the elephant of death.
>
> *HYP*, 2: 56

The *uḍḍīyāna bandha* is fully activated at the end of the exhalation with the breath held in retention. This diaphragmatic "flying up" can then be combined with *nauli kriyā*, or belly churning. This process is a cleansing technique, traditional for *haṭha yoga* practice, and is best done in the early morning before doing *āsana*. It is generally prescribed to improve digestion, problems with weight and over-eating and blockages in the *manipūraka chakra*.

To begin the practice of this *bandha* it is important that the belly be empty of food and liquid. It is better not to have a fever or be otherwise sick, particularly with headaches. It can be cleansing to do if one has a cold or mild flu. Breathe with a soft *ujjāyi*. Do not exaggerate the sound of the breath too much or you may get undue head pressure, headaches and faintness. If these symptoms occur do not persist. Build up on the exercise gradually.

Both hands are placed on either leg just above the knee. On the inhalation, look up slightly, arch the back and on the exhalation look down at the belly and round the back. The navel draws in towards the spine. Try to do this slowly rather than all in a rush. At this point the chin should be locked down (*jālandhara bandha*). Draw the diaphragm up, allowing as much expansion of the side ribs as possible. Make sure to breathe out fully first before flying upwards. Next, release the diaphragm and belly softly *and then* breathe in slowly without gasping. Avoid the tendency to drop the belly quickly and inhale abruptly as this will create undue head pressure. Initially hold the breath with the diaphragmatic lift for only three to four seconds. Slowly increase this time to approximately ten seconds.

Figure 18.

Uḍḍīyāna preparation: inhalation and exhalation.

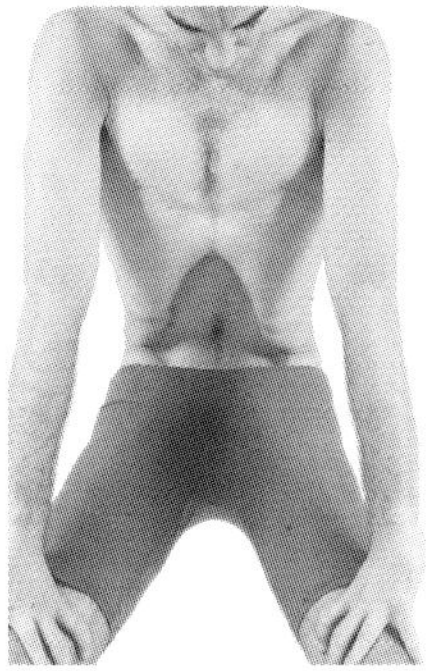

Uḍḍīyāna Bandha

Figure 19.

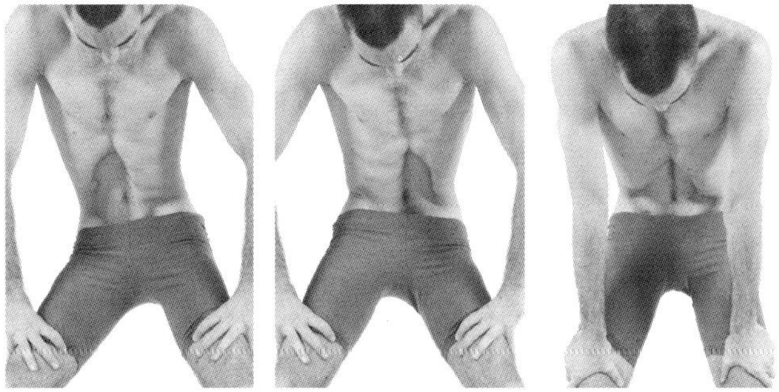

Nauli kriyā: right, left and centre.

Once the *uḍḍīyāna* process becomes stable, commence with *nauli kriyā*. This practice is the isolation of the side (right and left) and central muscles of the abdomen. Initially, it can be helpful to exaggerate the knee and hip movement in order to get some small isolation on one side. Eventually the control is all in the belly; the knees, hips and hands stay relatively still.

Begin to apply the *uḍḍīyāna bandha*. Start to press one hand and knee forward slightly, re-aligning the hips and pushing one side of the abdominal muscles forward. The other side of the abdomen remains drawn in. Alternate once or twice from side to side. It is useful to look at the belly - don't stay covered up with a shirt. Also, it is important to allow the belly to be quite fluid and soft with this process. A hard contracted abdomen does not move well. Once each side moves effectively, practice the fluid belly rolling, left to right and right to left. Rest between each retention. Finally, apply *uḍḍīyāna*, draw both sides in and activate the rectus abdominis through the centre. That is, contract the sides and push the centre forward, or at least release through the centre. (See figure 19.)

The practice of *uḍḍīyāna bandha* and *nauli kriyā* are useful in aiding lower back difficulty. It can be prescribed therapeutically for such problems as compressed lower spine, slipped discs and so on. The *uḍḍīyāna* is also prescribed to relieve blood congestion in the belly, excessive pulsing and pressure at the vena cava, menstrual pain and digestive problems such as constipation or diarrhoea. This *bandha* can help to regulate and balance a woman's moon cycle, but it can also easily hinder it. It should not be practiced during the menstrual period, particularly the three days prior to blood flow. If practiced excessively, particularly on the new moon, the *uḍḍīyāna* and *nauli* also tend to be aggravating. Listen to your body as some experimentation may be necessary. In some traditions this practice is not recommended for women at all; use your own discretion.

In the standard *vinyāsa* practice at no time is either the classic *uḍḍīyāna* (complete diaphragmatic lift) or *jālandhara bandha* (breath retention) used. It is the *mūla bandha* that is practiced throughout the *Aṣṭāṅga* sequence - and more commonly misunderstood. The general *uḍḍīyāna* movement should be encouraged on every inhalation. That is, lowering the diaphragm and so lengthening the spine. This is particularly useful in such postures as upward dog and *Vīrabhadrāsana A,* as controlling the diaphragm and rib movements decreases the impact on the lower back. Lowering the diaphragm and expanding the side ribs on the inhalation also increases *prāṇa* - this tends to engage *mūla bandha* automatically. Do the *uḍḍīyāna* and the *mūla bandha* will follow.

Through correctly applying the breath all three *bandha* are naturally maintained throughout the practice. It is not useful to hold the *bandha* rigidly, as this is usually a distraction from feeling what is truly going on. Neither should you ignore them. The breath should flow and move and so too the *bandha*.

The ambitions commonly associated with achieving the *āsana* are often mistakenly applied to achieving the *bandha*. The paradox of discipline versus relaxation may be a difficult one to resolve. It is limiting to assume that a more flexible or strong body is therefore more advanced in other ways. It only indicates the possibility of being more sensitive and aware rather than the certainty of it.

Also of note are the effects of ageing. The practice does suit younger, active people. It should become slower and steadier as the individual gets older. This may include holding the postures for longer periods of time, fewer jumping movements and more meditation. This does not mean, due to a lack of physical strength, that there is any lack of ability with the *bandha*. Although physical strength is desirable, such as that associated with the jump backs, it is not a particularly useful measure of gauging the *mūla bandha*. (See the three *granthi*, page 27).

Integrating Your Daily Practice

Learning the sequence is a lot like learning music. First you learn scales and repeat them, as per Salute to the Sun. Then you learn basic pieces of music such as the standing postures, and then complete compositions: the full Primary sequence and onwards to Intermediate etc. Some individuals may have the virtuoso talent to compose pieces themselves, but most will need advice from a teacher in order not to slide into the path of least resistance. There is a tendency to favour strengths and avoid weaknesses.

Practice begins in *Samasthitiḥ* with the *Aṣṭāṅga yoga mantra* (see page 35). It guides consciousness to the higher principles of *yoga*; the *Guru* within, the jungle physician removing the poison of conditioned existence (stanza one) and is an acknowledgment of the current line of teachers (stanza two) said to stem from Patanjali. The prayer is a little like taking the time to smell your food before eating: it aids the *āsana* digestion process. Practice finishes with the *mangala mantra* (see page 80), acknowledging the innate goodness in every human being. Although it describes both cows and *Brahmins* as being sacred, it indicates a universal principle: the sacredness of life. It is traditional to chant the final prayer in *Samasthitiḥ* after *Utpluthiḥ* and finishing in the same position that you started from. Although it is sometimes chanted between *Padmāsana* and *Utpluthiḥ*, to chant in between these two unnecessarily interrupts the practice. Another option is to chant the finishing mantra after taking rest when you are in a more relaxed frame of mind.

When first learning the Primary sequence try to practice at least three times per week. Do not overexert and take as much time as you need to develop your endurance. Gradually increase the weekly practice to five or six days with at least one day of rest. Having one day per week with a shorter practice is also beneficial - rather than either over-straining or not practising at all. Better thirty minutes every day than three hours once a week. Keep in mind that it is not necessary or desirable to practice every day. Try to maintain some consistency, but take a day or more of rest as the need arises. It is useful to watch how this affects the mind and body. Many students find the practice quite addictive. Learn also not to practice, though this may take years to understand.

There is a standard weekly routine for *Aṣṭāṅga* practice. The first day of practice is on Sunday and the last on Friday, with both Saturday and moon days (the full moon and the new moon) for rest. Saturday is governed by the planet Saturn, the planet of work, restriction and discipline. This planet is said to have the influence of being contractive, cold and dry. Therefore it is traditional not to practice on that day. Sunday is influenced by the Sun, considered to be the source of enlightenment. Monday is influenced by the moon, seen as a good day to start new ventures. Tuesday is influenced by Mars, god of war and fire. Due to the aggressive nature of Mars it is traditional not to give new postures on this day. Wednesday is influenced by Mercury, the planet of opposites, or mid-week duality. Thursday is influenced by Jupiter, planet of growth and unity, and Friday is influenced by Venus, goddess of love. Note: the deities represented here are equivalent in traditional Hindu mythology.

Each sequence of *Aṣṭāṅga yoga* is attached to a specific day of the week. For example, when first learning Intermediate, add those *āsana* to the Primary *āsana* on all days except Friday. The last day of practice is for Primary *āsana* only. When doing Intermediate on its own, however many *āsana*, you would practice it from Sunday to Thursday, Primary on Friday. When adding on Advanced *āsana* (A, B, C or D), Intermediate is practised on Sunday and Primary on Friday. Then from Monday to Thursday you would add Advanced A *āsana* to Intermediate, or practice Advanced (A, B, C or D) on its own. If the ability was there, then eventually you would begin the week with Intermediate (Sunday) and progress through Advanced A (Monday), Advanced B (Tuesday), Advanced C (Wednesday), Advanced D (Thursday) and finish with Primary (Friday). This process of learning and adding *āsana* is rarely straight forward. Most bodies have particular limitations. One particular sequence or one particular posture will restrict your ability to practice in the traditional manner, at least for a time. Finding ways to adapt the practice, or adapt yourself to the practice is a unique and creative process.

It is not at all necessary or desirable to do all of a sequence for it to be complete, or to feel complete on a bodily level. To attempt all of a sequence right from the start is often a matter of pushiness, trying to prove something. Or, it is a matter of guilt, for not having done enough or not feeling good enough. It takes time and discipline to develop endurance. When learning Intermediate for the first time it can be exhausting to add on new *āsana*. Attempt to do all of Primary, or as much as you have time for, before adding the Intermediate *āsana*. On one day per week you can practice Intermediate on its own, even if it is only the first four or five postures. Thursday is usually the best for this, sometimes called "research day". Generally it is good to start the week strongly and ease off towards the end of the week (finish with Primary as per the tradition).

As you add on more Intermediate *āsana* you can gradually decrease the Primary *āsana*. For example, do the Primary sequence up to *Baddha Koṇāsana* or *Marīchyāsana D* and add the Intermediate *āsana* after that. If the last part of your Primary sequence seems to be difficult, or remains uncoordinated, you have not been practising Primary for long enough and should avoid Intermediate until this section improves.

It is important not to avoid an *āsana* that is difficult. The guidelines for traditional practice are initially not only helpful but by and large essential. It is not a question of whether to stray from the traditional method, but when. Practice for years first; practice scales before trying to be a composer. Do not be in a hurry to reach the finish line, for there is none. By staying with what is occurring, no matter how difficult, change will inevitably result. From the traditional point of view, you simply do not move on to a new posture until the current one can be done properly. Different teachers do not always (or often) agree on what that is. Tradition can be a stumbling block if it is taken as the entirety of *yoga*. It is merely the wrapping in which it is presented.

There is a certain point in everybody's practice where some variation occurs, whether from injury, advice from a teacher, boredom or creative expression. Now and then it is useful to experiment, to move beyond the accepted form and play outside the square. If you are a beginner and are attempting to practice on you own, try to keep with the initial Primary *āsana* and seek a qualified teacher when possible. However, it is normal to try moving ahead and practice more difficult *āsana*. At some point just give it a go, even if the practice is a little rough around the edges. Do not fool yourself, however, that you are doing it correctly or that you have mastered a posture or a sequence when the reality might be quite different.

The level of your *yoga* is particularly obvious when you practice alone. The reliance on a teacher to adjust you into difficult *āsana* should be temporary. A teacher may often be necessary, but your greatest teacher is your own awareness. From the teacher's perspective each student should be gradually weaned from receiving strong or continual adjustments and be encouraged to maximise their own ability.

The test of self practice is when you can maintain it by yourself without external stimulation. Once you are beyond the beginning stage (usually the first two to three years of consistent practice) it is beneficial to practice for periods on your own. At other times seek a teacher or practice group as needed. Practising under a teacher or in a group does have its benefits, such as motivation, concentration and increased energy. Practising alone not only reveals your actual ability to do the postures, but also highlights any psychological difficulty. Initially you may tend to be more distracted and unmotivated without the teachers watchful eye. Solitary self practice is a practice of inner contemplation, self discipline and self reliance. A sign of a true *yogi* is being comfortable in your own skin - the ability to be alone.

Some *tapas*, or self discipline is necessary to keep the practice flowing and continuous, but you should also enjoy it! It takes no real discipline to come on to the *yoga* mat when you want to be there. If there is no liveliness to the practice it becomes lethargic. The breath becomes flat and uninspired. Enthusiasm is essential and should not be suppressed. Utilise your body's natural intelligence and find the balance between action and inaction, variation and consistency, inhalation and exhalation.

There is no doubt that some aspects of the sequence have changed. The practice has grown and evolved to suit the times. This does not deny the authenticity of the tradition, but the insistence that it has remained pure and unchanged for thousands of years. It has never suited everyone, nor was it meant for everyone. One change to the traditional sequence was the first posture of Intermediate. Originally it seems to have been *Malāsana*, or necklace posture. Its exclusion from the sequence remains a small mystery, one theory being that Intermediate had too many postures and Guruji was simplifying it. Another interesting change to the sequence is the location of *Ūrdhva Dhanurāsana*, the upward bow, or full bridge. In times past it seems that this posture was practised after *Karandavāsana* in the Intermediate sequence. Although it is now common to work on full bridge first, the initial back bending *āsana* in Intermediate tend to be easier and more therapeutic. Please note: although some of the changes to the traditional sequences have been documented in books and videos, they are difficult to directly confirm and must be considered as hearsay.

In Kṛiṣṇamacharya's time there were different ways in which the *vinyāsa* were practised. Often the *āsana* were linked together directly, one flowing into the next, such as *Paśchimottānāsana* into *Pūrvottanāsana* without jumping back in between. The West and East postures are also counterposes to each other, another reason to keep them flowing together. Kṛiṣṇamacharya was also known to link postures on one side all together, such as *Trikoṇāsana* into *Pārśvakoṇāsana* and so on. The regulation of jumping back (or up to *Samasthitiḥ*) from every posture does allow more consistency and helps to develop strength. However, there are possible drawbacks such as repetitive strain injury and boredom, both of these indicating a lack of awareness.

From the ideal *individual* and therapeutic approach to *yoga* that Kṛiṣṇamacharya advocated, modern *Aṣṭāṅga* can be overly regulated. The linear goal oriented nature of the practice often leads to an increased focus on achievement: who has a "better" practice or what is the correct practice. Conversely, not enough focus on the boundaries and tradition can also be a problem. The competitiveness that often arises is simply a stage, not one necessarily to be avoided; just something to pass through as you become more centred. The fiery nature of the practice also heightens awareness; the feeling is of moving forward. Eventually, however, there are only two possibilities: soften or bust. You either give up (or your body does) or you learn to relax into the reality of what is: self acceptance. The only correct practice is that which is, traditional practice or otherwise. You have the freedom to choose what is appropriate and you bear responsibility for that choice. It is your teacher's responsibility to direct you away from the path of least resistance towards the path of maximum benefit. Try to balance both of these inclinations.

Injuries and Rest

Injuries are a delicate issue and highly personal. When the body undergoes change intense sensations will often be present: acute bodily awareness. Eventually this will pass as a new alignment takes place. Sometimes an old injury from years past arises as practice is developed, an old pain coming to the surface. However, to pass off *all* pain as a bodily opening, or as stiffness in your mind is a mistake. Sharp pain is a very clear message of the body saying "Stop, enough!" You (or your teacher) may need to develop better awareness in order to distinguish between the different levels of sensation and pain.

It is all too common not to listen to the body until acute pain is present. As the sensory experience is developed then meaningful changes in movement can be made *before* acute pain arises. Listen to your body carefully. The teacher may point the way, but you are responsible for your choices. If you do experience increased pain modify your practice as necessary, rather than ignoring it and pushing through. Possibly this may mean stopping completely, alternatively it may mean continuing but at a greatly reduced pace.

Another cause for injury can be a teacher's tendency to over adjust in the attempt to get a student into a difficult posture. Initially some discomfort may need to be borne by the student in order to feel the completeness of the posture. Receiving an adjustment in a difficult *āsana* can be of great benefit. However, when a student is in pain this is definitely not advisable. If no pain is present the repetition of strong adjustments can still be counter productive, as this does not allow the student to find the space in the *āsana* for himself or herself.

During practice, mild discomforts such as faintness and cramping usually pass quickly. Drink plenty of fluid after every practice, but avoid drinking a lot beforehand and avoid drinking during the practice. However, if light headedness or cramping does persist in the midst of practice then drinking some fluid immediately is beneficial. Continuing to practice through the flu or a cold is generally possible, but rest if you have a high temperature or fever.

Some common areas for physical injuries are the hamstrings, lower back, knees, neck and shoulders. The first area, the hamstring, has the most potential to change. As stated previously this is a muscle and lengthens more readily than the denser material of tendon and bone. The hamstring injury can be common in the first year or so of practice. When the hamstring is injured near the insertion (at the top of the leg near the buttock) it may take between one and two years to heal. If the hamstring is injured lower down the leg it tends to heal in less than six months. Regular application of flaxseed oil to the area will help to keep the tissue softening.

Many students find that practising through a hamstring injury eventually works, though a gentle approach is best. It is useful to rest immediately after an injury, but to get back to your regular practice sooner rather than later is ideal. This does not mean pushing past the pain threshold but working with or meeting an injury in a way that is supportive.

With lower back injury there are a number of causes and a number of side effects, too many to enumerate here. The most common areas in the practice that affect the lower back are forward bends, back bends and twists. In the case of definite pain associated with forward bends, avoid receiving adjustments in such postures and focus on strengthening the whole body, particularly your abdomen. Slow down the *vinyāsa*, so that no movement is too fast or thoughtless. This brings greater awareness and injury decreases, healing increases. With back bend difficulty, strengthen the lower back, abdomen and the front of the legs. With drop backs the basic arching movement should be deliberately controlled rather than using flexibility alone. However, some perseverance through the initial discomfort of the drop back is what I recommend.

To start, the half-bend drop back can be practised in such a way that the abdomen becomes sore rather than the lower back. Try to utilise the front of the body and engage the psoas muscles to help control the arch. Do a number of half bend repetitions, but do not over do it. Gradually develop the strength necessary to do the full arch down to the floor. The psoas muscle contraction is not the same as the contraction of the *mūla bandha*, although it does tend to engage the pelvic floor. The psoas is to either side of the rectus abdominis and the *mūla bandha* rather than through the centre.

In the case of slipped discs, compressed vertebrae or the pinching of a nerve, extra physical therapy may be necessary. All injuries have deeper psychological traits and tendencies. Such problems (physical and psychological) should not be avoided and may need to be addressed with other therapeutic approaches. The knees are a common weak point in the human anatomy, particularly the meniscus, the inward area of the joint. If there is any swelling in the knee joint (or any joint) excessive heat, whether internal or external, should be avoided until the swelling reduces. That is, do not practice until the joint becomes more mobile.

It is common that stiffness in the hips and lower spine translates into pressure on the knee. Work slowly with the practice and focus on the centre of the body particularly the groin, hips and sacrum. If the hips and spine become more supple and stable, knee pressure will gradually decrease. If they do not, then keep decreasing the pressure on the knees rather than increasing it. If the meniscus is badly torn then seek further advice from a medical professional. If the ligaments or tendons to the knee are damaged, generally this will improve with time and steady, gradual practice.

The neck is a sensitive area and relatively fragile. Do not push into pain in this area. Due to the jumps in the standard sequence, it can be difficult to modify the practice with a shoulder or wrist injury. Try to engage the latisimus dorsi (side muscles) of the trunk and the abdominal muscles, rather than placing pressure on the shoulders and neck. The latter may be quite common when you are beginning, particularly pressure to the trapezius muscle. Try to keep your shoulder blades generally downwards throughout the practice, and your elbows tucked in when you jump back. Keep your back, side and front ribs spacious without over expanding them. Injury of the wrist is usually linked to shoulder difficulty. A simple outward turning of the hand in down dog and upward dog helps a great deal if the wrist is sore: have the index finger pointing forward rather than the middle finger.

The use of props (blocks, bolsters, straps, wall etc.) often becomes attractive in the midst of an injury or particular difficulty. Props are often useful to increase awareness of your blind spots and as an aid to relaxation. However, as far as the tradition is concerned, they should be used sparingly, if at all. In the middle of a flowing practice most props are disruptive and largely unnecessary. The continuity of awareness will be lost and the prop can easily become a crutch rather than a stepping stone. This includes adding variations to a posture before actually practising e.g. to open the shoulders before doing back bends or to open the hips before doing legs-behind-the-head. The warm up attitude is often about non-acceptance. Practice with continuity.

With all injuries, do not push past the pain threshold. Regular practice should be approached with a therapeutic attitude. Do not ignore the body's obvious signals. Respect your pain, work with it and meet it half way. Apply flaxseed oil and castor oil as needed. Flaxseed oil aids tissue regrowth and castor oil breaks down scar tissue. Getting regular therapeutic massage can also help. Try to avoid having the spine cracked and manipulated too often. These are invasive measures and some discretion is required to decide when they are useful. Give the body the time it needs to heal and allow the practice to work for you: accept your body as it is, not as you want it to be.

The ability to rest and sleep deeply at the appropriate time is vital for healing. It is not necessarily the practice of *āsana* that causes change: it is while in a more relaxed state that the body realigns itself to a new configuration. Of course, if you do not practice, no new configuration is possible. Likewise for *prāṇāyāma*. It is difficult to deepen awareness in a meaningful way without some trigger or technique. Taking sufficient rest at the end of the practice is often overlooked. Do not rush off your mat to go to work, try to allow at least twenty minutes lying on your back. Do not get up: relax or fall asleep.

Oversleeping tends to stiffen the body. An increase in *tamasic* or sluggish energy slows the metabolic rate. However, the mind tends to be calmer. Not sleeping as much tends to promote flexibility, the *rajasic* or active energy keeps the metabolic rate higher. However, there is usually a corresponding drop in strength if the system does not receive enough rest. There is a danger in both of these extremes. Each individual should balance these poles as appropriate.

Almost all meditative traditions (East and West) advocate contemplation in the hours before dawn. In the *yoga* tradition it is believed that the hours between 3am and 5am are the most beneficial for *āsana*, *prāṇāyāma* and meditation. This time is called *brahmamuhurta*, considered to be the most *sattvic*, or balanced, tranquil and sacred period. It may take some discipline to become acclimatised to this time of day. However, if getting up at 3am results in exhaustion, extreme weight loss, anxiety and/or anti social behaviour, then sleeping for longer is advisable. A good attitude and a happy smile are far more important. Practice between 5am and 9am is also suitable, as long as you do not skip breakfast. It is not recommended to practice *Aṣṭāṅga yoga* in the evening. In particular you should avoid strong back bends after the sun has set, otherwise headaches, heart palpitations, kidney pain and/or insomnia may result. It is helpful to get to sleep well before the midnight hour (between 9pm and 10pm is best) when the nervous system should be least disturbed. Therefore it is also best to eat the evening meal between 5.30pm and 6.30pm to allow time for digestion.

The climate in which you practice also has an obvious effect. As it is much easier (and more relaxing) for the body to open in a warmer climate, practising *āsana* at 5am in colder climates may be inadvisable, if not seemingly impossible, without a great deal of artificial heat. In an overly humid climate practising at dawn or before is generally the best option in order to avoid over sweating and draining the body of essential fluids. It is considered beneficial to rub your sweat back into your skin just after practice, to reabsorb lost nutrients.

Food and Sex

Nourishing, healthy food is important. A vegetarian diet with as much variety as possible is generally advisable, or at least considered beneficial to the practice of *yogāsana*. It encourages a lighter and more flexible constitution. Vegetarianism also promotes sensitivity, though if you are changing from a typical meat-based diet you may initially feel a little ungrounded and light headed. Ideally the food should be organic, in season and locally grown. Above all, eat consciously, eat slowly. The food will taste better and will be absorbed more completely. Food should be an enjoyment, though not an indulgence.

One particular problem with diet and *yoga* is the moral stance of being vegetarian. That is, you are not a real *yogi*, or not a good or kind human being if you eat meat! Eating meat does not automatically relegate an individual to a lower spiritual status. Some diets are simply more appropriate or supportive than others. For some women during menstruation the loss of blood can cause an anaemic reaction. Eating meat may be a more balanced option, particularly for women with hormonal and blood sugar issues.

In my opinion the advantages of being vegetarian generally outweigh the disadvantages, as long as there is enough variation in the diet and a willingness to change it with the location and the seasons. All diet regimes around the world have a particular, and usually cultural, bias. Each one has advantages, such as that promoted in *Ayurveda* (traditional Indian medicine), for *yoga* practitioners. But, if you do not come from that particular culture there may be some drawbacks. Be very careful of accepting a particular diet when you are not in its country of origin. It is generally accepted that the food you take should be *sattvic*, or balanced, neither stimulating nor heavy. No two systems will ever agree on what is actually a balanced diet. Learn to experiment.

Nutrition, particularly in relation to spiritual practice, is often an emotionally charged subject. It is not surprising that this has lead to, or leads from, various eating disorders. Regarding diet attempt to listen to the needs of your body, rather than emotional or psychological needs. Food is for the body; your mental, emotional and spiritual needs should be nourished by other sources. Some discipline is usually necessary to establish and co-ordinate these seemingly opposing forces. For some individuals the habit and conflict with food and self image may be so severe that a balanced attitude is impossible. That is, the perception that you have of your "healthy diet" is at odds with reality. Support through either medical, psychiatric or alternate therapies may be necessary.

I have observed that a highly restricted and controlled diet often results in a conflicting self image. Any increase in physical health will tend to be outweighed by neurotic tendencies. However, there should be some attention to your diet rather than none at all. Be aware and listen to the needs of your body. This includes the possibility of supporting the system with various supplements, vitamins and minerals. If the purpose of practice is to increase self awareness then the support from your diet and practice should be mutual. Your diet should not decrease your ability to practice, but neither should your practice become so all consuming that your diet becomes limited and overly controlled.

Another area of concern is the bowel movement first thing in the morning. Commonly if there is no bowel movement practice can be quite uncomfortable. Having a lighter meal in the evening may be one option. In most traditions, however, the colon is the organ most likened to stubbornness and the inability to let go and allow change. The more relaxed you are, the more likely for the colon to release. If practising causes an increase in tension, holding on, sleeplessness, and hunger and so on then it is hardly likely that the overall benefits are good. It is not what you do that is most important; it is your relationship to it that really matters.

Some individuals also like to drink coffee first thing in the morning, both to aid the bowel movement and to wake up from feeling tired. That is, coffee is used to do both these things rather than actually addressing the issue. First of all, the question of why you are tired should be addressed. Secondly, if you are, either go to sleep earlier or practice later. If you drink coffee to help practice, then it can be said that what goes to practice is not you, it is the coffee. My point here is not to condemn coffee. It is a part of life and may be relatively supportive. I use it here as an example of the illusions you have that may need to be addressed.

It is traditional to practice *yoga* in conjunction with *kriyā* or cleansing routines. They include such processes as fasting, nasal cleansing, belly churning and colon purification. The *kriyā* help to purify the body and tend to make stretching easier. That is, as your muscles begin to eliminate toxins, they lose their harder, contracted quality. However, there is usually a corresponding drop in strength and energy as some of the good goes out with the bad. Do not over do it! The two aspects of accumulation and elimination need to be balanced in order to gain the full benefit from your system.

Personal regimes such as fasting and *brahmacharya* (celibacy) can be helpful as an aid to increase awareness and to understand addiction, but are also potentially extreme. Periodic fasting should decrease the negative impact that food has when you do eat. By fasting you should become less emotionally attached to food, rather than more - though eating should not become devoid of enjoyment and purely mechanical. Food is life!

It is common after fasting to become either obsessive about eating healthy food, or the reverse, over indulgent. The tendency to control all aspects of your life through food (or fasting) should be avoided. When the digestion process becomes healthier it becomes devoid of undue emotion, positive or negative. It is not what you eat; it is your relationship to it that matters. Fasting and *brahmacharya* are practices of *vairāgya*, detachment and openness, rather than denial and suppression.

The wider your polarities the higher your neurosis. The more integrated your polarities, the lower your neurosis. The so called narrow *yogic* path is not one of complete restriction. It is of walking between your polarities, rather than rapidly swinging from one to the other. The Buddha Siddhartha once likened the playing of the Sitar with the play of life: "If the string is too loose one cannot play. Too tight and it breaks."

This does not imply that eating junk food is desirable; use some discretion. This is particularly true for various stimulants and intoxicants. Manufactured drugs (prescribed and illegal), cigarettes, marijuana, alcohol, coffee and particularly heavy foods all stimulate the nervous system in various ways. Such substances generally suppress your body's natural tendencies and your capacity to be aware. However, deciding whether it is more or less supportive to use such things is delicate. For example, if medical intervention decreases a neurotic, conflicted state then this is generally advisable. For many physical conditions a medical procedure and/or medication of some kind is definitely appropriate.

Sexual issues vary for every individual. It is your relationship to your own particular sexual process that should become clearer whether you engage in intercourse, masturbation or celibacy. Each individual should work with their own unique sexual process. By understanding and integrating the full power of your sexual drive and desires, you will no longer be manipulated by your own hidden, unconscious and conflicting needs: self-expression rather than self-suppression.

For a man, there may be a need for increased sexual control, whether in complete abstinence or in delayed ejaculation. To an extent greater control is useful, but this should always be tempered by an ability to let go and surrender to the natural process. The masculine is empowered through surrender to and fulfilment of his own primal energy. Focus on the process rather than the goal. The sexual experience for a man usually culminates with *apānic* elimination: ejaculation. If this is over indulged then tiredness, depletion or exhaustion may result. The *āsana* practice should help with both sexual control and an increase in energy that supports the sexual process. During intercourse pay attention to the perineal area, the *mūla bandha* and your breath. Accentuate the upward movement of your energy on the inhalation. You can also include various pelvic floor/meditation exercises as a part of your daily routine. (See page 84, Mantak Chia).

By becoming aware of the base two *chakra*, and the ability to feel the energy moving along the central channel, you can begin to practice what is called the microcosmic orbit, of channelling the physical sexual energy to the higher centres. (Refer to the seven *chakra*, page 24). Various effects such as increased sensitivity, waves of bliss and heightened states of consciousness may begin to manifest. Almost as a side effect, the capacity to orgasm without ejaculation will become possible. This does not imply that ejaculation (or masturbation) is in any way wrong. It is becoming *conscious* of this letting go process and its consequences that will make a difference. You will be less inclined to be reactive and engage in sex or masturbation due to stress or incapacity to relate and more inclined to be pro-active and expressive. The cultivation of sexual energy is a creative and powerful process. It is interesting to note that the phases of the moon have a definite effect on ejaculation and sexual retention (see Moon Days below).

In many traditions it is said that a man will age prematurely if he does not learn to control or reduce ejaculation. It can also be said that you are inevitably going to grow old and die and that attempting to completely halt the natural process is egotistical, also resulting in ill-health. To orgasm without ejaculation should not become an all-consuming goal. To strive for it will tend to create further imbalances. The development of the sexual *kumbhaka* is a product of right-relationship: the willingness to be truly yourself, in your own sexual power, and to be receptive and open to your sexual partner. Through practice and right relationship you can manifest both sexual retention (control) and multiple sustained orgasms (letting go). This is divine life force at play in the body. These yogic sexual practices may take years to evolve, if at all. They are a part of the awakening of *kuṇḍalinī*, the primal energy. Although these practices may seem far-fetched, with consistent awareness and openness to the process they are possible for anyone.

Due to the standard Sunday to Friday practice of *Aṣṭāṅga yoga*, some male practitioners limit their sexual activity to Friday night, as there is no practice on Saturday. Friday being the day of Venus, Goddess of love, this would seem appropriate. That is, no sex during the week so that you can practice with greater energy. This artificial restriction often indicates a difficulty with relating in a sexual manner, both to others and to oneself. Your sexual process should support your practice, rather than limit it. Your *āsana* practice should support your sexual process.

The practice of *brahmacharya* is undeniably useful; particularly to understand your own sexual tensions and your relationship to others. Periodic celibacy can increase awareness of sexual *prāṇa* and tends to increase the energy flow to the higher centres. To repeat, it is a practice of awareness and observation, rather than control and restriction. *Brahmacharya* is translated as "teacher of the soul".

For women, intercourse combines both *prāṇa* (intake) and *apāna* (discharge). The four basic phases of the moon greatly influence the degree to which a woman is feeling sexual. The *āsana* practice should support and coincide with each of these phases, with a slightly (or greatly) different emphasis for each. (See Moon Days below).

With improved practice, also including various pelvic floor/meditation exercises, a woman can increase her awareness of menstruation and ovulation. Both of these cycles will become more refined and ideally pain free. In particular, the depletion of energy associated with the loss of blood will become less and less. Blood flow should still occur (until menopause) but without the negative physical and mental side effects. Do not focus solely on the menstruation aspect of the cycle. Place equal emphasis on ovulation. As your awareness of both halves of your cycle increases your system will harmonise.

During intercourse pay more attention to the cervix, the *mūla bandha* and the ovaries. Accentuate the upward movement of your energy on the inhalation. Through awareness of this lower region and the lower two *chakra*, you can begin to access the microcosmic orbit, channelling your sexual energy to the higher centres. (See figure 22, page 25). As you begin to balance a healthy sense of your own boundaries with surrender to your own primal energy, right-relationship manifests. That is, as you begin to fully trust yourself, trust in your sexual partner will then develop correspondingly.

The integration of your lunar polarities is the feminine aspect of raising *kuṇḍalinī*. Sexually this will tend to manifest as multiple, sustained orgasms. (Refer to bibliography, page 84, Mantak Chia). The combination of the refined masculine and feminine sexual process co-creates more choices regarding sexual activity and conception.

The *āsana* practice can adversely affect your sexual capacity. Through continuous practice, profuse sweating and intense concentration, you might often feel tired, depleted and unmotivated sexually. Alternatively you may feel a heightened sense of sexuality and be tempted to perceive the practice in a purely sexual manner. These are passing phases, but if they persist it is important to either change the practice, or at least change your attitude to the practice. Do not use the practice as an escape from dealing with what is, from dealing with your own sexual and sensual issues. Come into contact with your own sexual experience and enjoy the process as it is.

Moon Days, Women and Weight Loss

It is traditional not to practice *āsana* on the full moon or the new moon. The days preceding the full moon cause an increase in fluid in the body, an internal tide, and generally an increase in energy. As this tends to cause over stimulation, intense practice is not recommended. The days preceding the new moon (sometimes called the dark moon) cause a decrease in fluids in the body. As a tendency there will be less energy, the joints more dry and so an increased chance of injury. Of the two it is less problematic to practice on the full moon rather than the new moon. The twenty four hours preceding the exact time that the moon is at its peak (brightest or darkest) is the day not to practice. That is, if the moon is full at 2.04am on Monday, do not practice on the Sunday before. At 2.05am the moon is already waning and so practice after 2.04am on Monday is advisable.

The waning of the moon (becoming darker) is a reducing, eliminating, *apānic* process. The peak of the dark moon is a time to start new ventures and it is renewing. The waxing of the moon (becoming brighter) is an increasing, accumulating, *prāṇic* process. It is a time for activity and consolidation. Pay attention to the phases of the moon and become aware of these effects on your body. This should be real rather than imagined! Do not pretend that the moon has no influence on you, whether you are male or female.

For most women there is a tendency to menstruate or ovulate on either the full or the new moon. The full moon is accumulating; the increase of blood (menstruation) may be common at that time. The new moon is renewing, the downward flow of energy or blood (menstruation) may also be common at this time. There is no strict rule as to what is most appropriate. For some women it may not be at either of those times. Groups of women living together tend to find their cycles more likely to coincide with each other and the moon. There is a tendency to gain weight prior to menstruation and prior to the full moon. There is a tendency to lose weight just after menstruation and just prior to the new moon. The temptation to fast or purge just prior to the period (when feeling heavier) should be avoided as it impedes the natural process. A gentle cleanse just after the period is considered more appropriate.

It is inadvisable for women to practice the full *Aṣṭāṅga* sequence for the first three days of menstruation. For some either a modified sequence (avoiding inversions, extreme backbends and certain twisting postures) or a completely alternative sequence is useful. Refer to bibliography, *Chandra Moon Sequence*, page 84. Others may decide that complete rest for two or three days is what they need. One way to approach this is to practice only passive postures on the first day of the period, such as *Supta Vīrāsana,* and then sticking your legs up the wall and resting there. On the second day add some of the basic standing postures and a few other sitting postures, particularly those that open the hips. On the third day practice a gentle version of the Primary sequence. Do not ignore your cycle and attempt to practice the full *Aṣṭāṅga* sequence straight through it!

It is also inadvisable to attempt any of the classic locks (*bandha*) during the period as this tends to restrict the downward course of the blood. This is particularly true of *uḍḍīyāna bandha* and *nauli kriyā*. During the three days prior to menstruation these practices should also be avoided. Gentle *prāṇāyāma* without retention is therapeutic during the menstrual cycle. It is important not to do vigorous cleansing or elimination on the new moon (for men and women) as this can cause excessive depletion. For example: fasting, most of the *kriyā*, sauna, ejaculation, or any exercise that causes profuse sweat. A man should become aware of the different effects that the full and new moon have on ejaculation, just as a woman does for menstruation and ovulation.

Some women experience a complete absence of cycle for a time. This is largely due to the intensity of the practice, profuse sweat and sudden weight loss. The absence of menstruation should not continue for longer than about six months without being attended to, though there are usually few problems for this duration. If the period does remain absent, or difficult, make every attempt to give your cycle and the phases of the moon more space and attention in your life. Try to allow the practice to be more cooling with softer breathing and movements. Take at least two days off practice each week and two days rest around each of the moon days to begin realigning with the moon's rhythms. If you are lean or underweight try to gain weight - soft tissue and fat rather than muscles. A qualified herbalist can also be of help in bringing the menstrual cycle back into balance.

During pregnancy the practice should be modified with each successive trimester. A great deal will depend on the current state of your *yoga*. If you have a strong, committed practice then there is usually no harm in continuing. Your body will be used to it, so practice is unlikely to disrupt the pregnancy. However, during the first trimester it is often recommended either to limit the practice or not to practice at all due to increasing nausea and the fragile status of the foetus. You can then increase your practice in the second trimester and reduce it again with the third. It is important to listen to the needs of your body and respond accordingly. Common sense should dictate what is appropriate. As your abdomen becomes larger, postures that twist or compress the belly should be omitted. Postures that open the hips and strengthen the legs and spine can be maintained throughout. The headstand can be beneficial as it will tend to aid the movement of the foetus and therefore encourage the correct position for delivery. Be aware, however, as the baby grows and your centre of balance changes this can adversely affect any inverted or balancing *āsana*. If you have not been practising for long, focus primarily on the standing postures, easy back bends and upright *Baddha Koṇāsana*. Consult your *yoga* teacher and/or medical professional for further advice.

If there are difficulties falling pregnant, the intensity of the practice should be reduced and the number of postures decreased until the sequence is suitably gentle. If you tend to be lean or underweight an increase in body fat will usually be of benefit. Lastly, try to follow the rhythm of the moon a little more closely and take rest on the moon days if you are not already.

A common problem of *Aṣṭāṅga yoga* is that it can adversely reduce your weight. As your musculature and structure lengthen, loss of body fat also tends to occur. However, because excessive or continued weight loss causes dryness in the body and a lack of soft tissue, ill health may also result. This is particularly true for women. If a woman does not have at least a small layer of fat optimum health is unlikely. The tendency to be driven and to keep pushing in the practice at the expense of a relaxed state of mind and body should be avoided. The practice should always be supportive for your body type. Being lean or underweight, or overly muscular, are simply stages that some bodies go through. Due to the progressive nature of *Aṣṭāṅga yoga* there can be a desire to be that way in order to perform better in the *āsana*. This indicates a lack of self acceptance and a negative attitude to the body. Maintaining this attitude is undesirable: the bodily condition may come and go, it is your ability to stay present and balanced that is crucial.

The changes in your body and the emotions that go with it are strongly affected by the phases of the moon. For example, tense and over-anxious on the full moon, depleted and depressed on the new moon. Keep a moon diary and note the seasonal changes. Be aware of self-fulfilling prophecies, do not pre-program yourself. Respect the phases of the moon and move with the tide.

One criticism of *Aṣṭāṅga yoga* is that the practice was intended for *Brahmin* boys rather than women. The practice can be a problem in cases of physical depletion, negative body image and excessive pushiness. This can be, or should be of equal concern for men. However, the sequence also provides a combination of strength and flexibility and it can support a man or woman equally. Generally there are more women than men practising *yoga*, particularly the Primary sequence. However, there are almost an equal number of men and women who finish the Intermediate sequence and there seems to be more men who finish Advanced. The flexibility required in the first sequence seems to exclude more men, but the strength required in the following sequences seems to exclude more women. The sequence may not be possible for everyone, but neither should it be totally unapproachable. Some leeway is necessary to allow room for each student to express herself or himself without collapsing the core principles of the practice.

The Seven *Chakra*

There are seven principle *chakra*, an esoteric system of wheels within wheels. Each of these wheels forms the different levels of our nature, with each of the seven having their own individual levels. The *chakra* are probably best described with analogy or poetry, for the truth is layered.

The manifest Self is a three-part being consisting of body, emotion and mind. The friction caused by the interaction of these primary aspects creates another three secondary, derived aspects. The interaction of mind and body has a particular dynamic and friction. It is typically masculine, survival driven and fiery. The interaction of body and emotion is typically feminine, nurturing and watery. The interaction of mind and emotion is non-sexual, non-physical and focused towards purity and higher love. The energy (un-manifest Self) or spirit that pervades all six is the seventh aspect. Thus there are seven spheres.

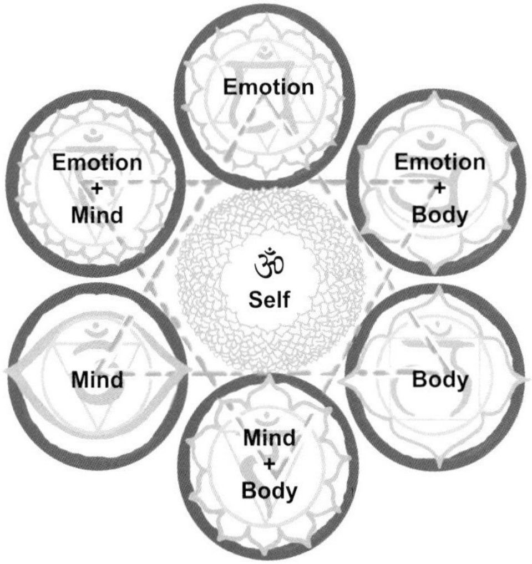

Figure 20. Sapta Chakra Maṇḍala.

The upright triangle contains primary characteristics:

Body - *mūlādhāra chakra*
Emotion - *anāhata chakra*
Mind - *ājñā chakra*

The downward triangle contains secondary/derived characteristics:

Emotion/body - *svādiṣṭhāna chakra* (Sexuality - feminine)
Mind/body - *maṇipūraka chakra* (Survival - masculine)
Emotion/mind - *viśuddha chakra* (Purity - asexual)

Each *chakra* is depicted as a lotus flower or *padma*. This flower grows out of the mud, balances perfectly on water and is nourished by air and sun. The purity of the lotus (despite its mud-like origin) conveys both delicacy and stability or *sukha* and *sthira*. The central aspect of the *maṇḍala* is spirit, the non-dualistic integrated Self. Spirit is feeling based, or "felt one-ness with being". It occurs as emotion in the manifest self and is situated at the top of the pyramid. Although it is more common to arrange these spheres vertically (figure 21), this can be perceived as purely linear (step one, step two, step three etc.) The spheres are analogous of a DNA spiral: each one connects directly with all the others. The vertical arrangement of the *chakra* are akin to rungs on a ladder, or climbing upwards. The state of *samadhi*, or spirit consciousness, is of jumping off the ladder entirely and taking flight. It is important to make sure you are high enough, and that you have wings, otherwise you will break your legs when you fall! The ladder, although it is

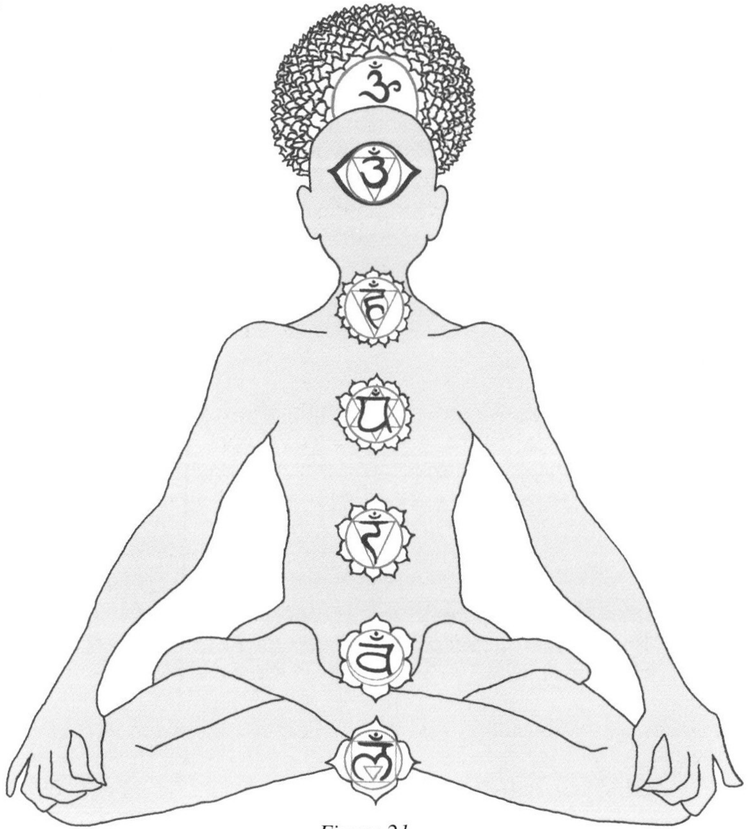

Figure 21.

7 *Sahasrāra:*	True self	1000 petalled lotus, liberation.
6 *Ājñā:*	Ego-less	To perceive, insight.
5 *Viśuddha:*	Substance-less	Purity, refined ether.
4 *Anāhata:*	Air	Un-struck, open and without form.
3 *Maṇipūraka:*	Fire	City of gems, provider of energy.
2 *Svādiṣṭhāna:*	Water	Sweetness, moon, womb.
1 *Mūlādhāra:*	Earth	Root foundation, body.

The first six *chakra* are located as follows: *mūlādhāra* at the perineum (relating to the prostatic plexus), *svādiṣṭhāna* at the tip of the tail-bone (sacral plexus), *maṇipūraka* above the navel (relating to the solar plexus), *anāhata* at the heart (cardiac plexus), *viṣuddha* at the throat (larynginal plexus), *ājñā* between the two eyebrows (cavernous plexus). The seventh, *sahasrāra* is located on and above the crown of the head and connects the individual soul (*ātman*) with the infinite (*Brahman*). Each of the wheels stem from the *suṣumṇā nāḍī*, the central nerve of the non-dualistic Self. It is important to understand that each wheel higher in the chain encapsulates the previous wheel rather than being separate to it; circles within circles. At no time are they divorced, each one is

Figure 22.

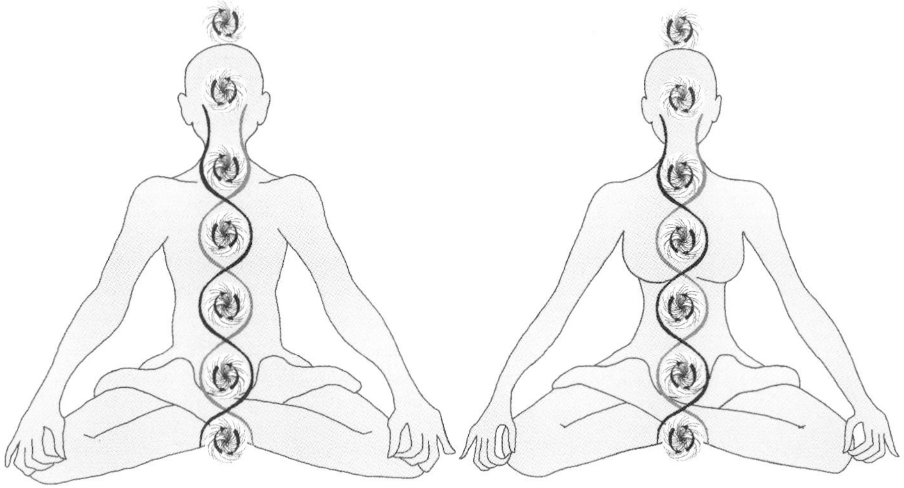

Chakra	Petals (1)	*Mantra* (2)	*Yantra* (3)	Colour (4)	Male/Female (5)	Planet (6)	*Yoga* (7)
Sahasrāra	1008	*Aum*	Formless	Violet	CW ACW	Neptune	*Rāja*
Ājñā	96	*Kṣam*	Infinity	Indigo	ACW CW	Uranus	*Jñāna*
Viśuddha	16	*Ham*	Lotus	Blue	CW ACW	Saturn	*Mantra*
Anāhata	12	*Yam*	Star	Green	ACW CW	Jupiter	*Bhakti*
Maṇipūraka	10	*Ram*	Triangle	Gold	CW ACW	Mars	*Karma*
Svādiṣṭhāna	6	*Vam*	Crescent	Orange	ACW CW	Venus	*Tantra*
Mūlādhāra	4	*Lam*	Square	Red	CW ACW	Mercury	*Haṭha*

Petals. Like a bicycle wheel in motion each *chakra* appears to have a few spokes or many depending on its speed. The higher the energy, the higher the *chakra* and the number of its petals increases exponentially. Note: the sixth *chakra*, *ājñā*, is typically portrayed with two petals, but each of these has forty-eight divisions making ninety-six petals in total.

***Mantra*.** Each *mantra*, or any sound for that matter, creates a resonance in the body and along the spine. The vibration of a particular *mantra* is said to activate a particular *chakra*. If a *mantra* is repeated with awareness then the awareness of each *chakra* increases. Also, base and baritone vibrations accentuate the base *chakra,* and the higher vibrations, soprano and alto accentuate the higher *chakra*. The syllable *aum* is considered to be the most sacred and universal sound. *Aum* (*om* ॐ) is made up of three distinct sounds; *aa*, *au* and *ma,* creating a vibration that traverses up the spine. *Aa* represents creation at the base *chakra* (*Brahmā*), *au* represents preservation at the heart *chakra* (*Viṣnu*) and *ma* represents destruction at the third eye (*Śiva*).

***Yantra*.** A *yantra* is a shape or geometric pattern that sustains concentration on a subtle level. The first primal *yantra* is a dot, the *bindu* that begins all creation. The square is the first structure of the human animal, that is the *mūlādhāra chakra*. The crescent moon, the womb of Self, is a circle that touches each side from within the square. This denotes the second *chakra*. The downward pointing triangle is the masculine principle, or the third *chakra*. The *bindu* is considered to be at the lower apex of this triangle. The combination of the two triangles into a six pointed star unites both masculine and feminine principles in the heart *chakra*. The lotus flower of the fifth *chakra* denotes purity, the refinement of the individual's essence. The oval shape of the sixth *chakra* is also portrayed as the infinity figure-eight symbol relating to insight. The *sahasrāra chakra* has no form.

Colour. The colour of each *chakra*, as per the human visible spectrum, changes from red to violet. The tones of these colours vary from individual to individual. This upward change in colour is similar to the red shift explained in Western science: as an object in space moves away with great speed, its colour appears more red, as an object moves closer it appears more blue.

Male and Female. The rotation of each *chakra* alternates one by one from clockwise (CW) to anti-clockwise (ACW). Men and women (or masculine/feminine) alternate differently. For example, the *mūlādhāra* spins clockwise and the *svādiṣṭhāna* anti clockwise for the masculine. For the feminine *mūlādhāra* spins anti clockwise and *svādiṣṭhāna* clockwise. The combination of clockwise/anti-clockwise spin creates the possibility of sexual harmony; "felt one-ness with being."

Planet. Each of the planets in the solar system forms greater spheres of influence, linked to the inner ones. As above, so below. The planetary chain is completely encompassed by the power of the sun. It represents divine consciousness, the light that touches and purifies everything. The planet Earth represents the manifest Self, individual consciousness in its myriad forms. The moon represents illusion, man's nature that is obscured from consciousness. The "dark side of the moon" is symbolic (though some say it is literal) as the home of demons, the detritus of man's lower nature which is obscured from the light of the sun.

In the planetary chain Mercury is first from the sun. It is the planet of movement and is likened to *haṭha yoga*. Mercury is also dualistic, hot and cold, and juxtaposed between the sun and moon (*ha/ṭha*). The planet Venus (feminine) is connected to the second *chakra* and the planet Mars (masculine) to the third. Venus is more inward (both as a planet and as an energy) and nurturing. Mars is more outward and is concerned with survival. When the feminine principle is out of balance (body + emotion = lack of concentration), it is common for it to manifest in the masculine zone, e.g. eating disorders. When the masculine principle is out of balance (mind + body = lack of emotional awareness) it manifests in the female zone, e.g. sexuality. Jupiter governs growth and unity of purpose (heart), Saturn governs seriousness, inner authority and restriction (throat). When Saturn is unbalanced (mind + emotion = lack of bodily awareness), generally through too much talking or too much thinking, the body becomes unwell. Uranus governs break-throughs and insight (third eye), and Neptune governs the ideal, is permeating and without boundaries (crown of the head).

***Yoga*.** Each of the different forms of *yoga* are also likened to each of the wheels. No matter which method of *yoga* is practiced, one way or another it affects all of the other levels. Meditation is governed by *rāja yoga.* Knowledge and the study of sacred scripture is *jñāna yoga.* Prayer and chanting is governed by *mantra yoga.* Love and devotion is governed by *bhakti yoga.* Food and work is governed by *karma yoga.* Sexual and creative energy is governed by *tantra yoga* (also called *kuṇḍalinī yoga*). Body duality is governed by *haṭha yoga.* Athough each *chakra* is more refined than the one below it, the *anāhata* is the heart of the system. It is at the top of the *chakra maṇḍala*. It lies to the exact centre of the seven *chakra*, three above, three below. It is the heart that connects all of the others and all endeavour comes back to the heart. Thus, of all the *yogas* it is said that *bhakti* (devotion) brings one immediately to God. The heart connects all the aspects of Self, all beings and all things. In the *chakra* system the Self is said to reside in the heart.

The current era we live in is said to be of the third *chakra,* typically a masculine age, focused towards work and achievement, or *karma yoga*, and of the element fire. The previous era is said to be of the second *chakra*, was more feminine, nurturing and of the element water. The interaction of mind and body (masculine) is limited if it does not involve emotional understanding. The current growth of all human beings is towards the heart, the fourth *chakra*. This shift from the gross, lower body and the three base *chakra* to the heart centre is a radical evolution. The third sphere is the "city of gems", or city of the sun (*pūraka*) and is evolving towards the "unstruck bell", the silent sound within every heart: the emotional centre of the fourth sphere. The only true emotion is love, all others stem from a block or denial of love. This does not invalidate other emotions, but acknowledges their impermanent nature. This is the formless purity of love; love is the present moment, love is change.

The Five *Vāyu* and Three *Dośa*

Each of the seven *chakra* pertains to the elemental forces of the body and of nature (figure 23). As above, so below: the inner world of an individual is a reflection of the outer world. The elemental regions of the body are called *vāyu*, literally meaning air. They describe the "airy" vital forces of the body. That is, the physical nature is in a constant state of flux despite its seeming solidity. Earth is an inward force and contracts to keep things together. Water is a downward force and eliminates the unwanted. Fire is an upward force, is transforming, and consumes everything in its path. Air is an outward force which attempts to enter anything it touches. Ether has no physical manifestation and pervades everything. The five *vāyu* are a *process* rather than a *state*. Every moment is born out of the previous one, grows old and dies, only to be born again in a new form. Earth is eroded by water, but also contains it. Water is evaporated by fire, but also douses it. Fire is blown out with air, but also consumes it. Air is directed by ether and is the vehicle through which it experiences. Ether manifests in all things.

Each of the five elements should be balanced within each aspect of the *yoga* practice. Standing postures deal with the skeleton, the legs and arms. That is, *vyāna*, the earth element. Prone postures, particularly resting at the end of practice, deal with *apāna*, the water element, and are more cooling. Sitting postures deal mostly with the mid-section, are generally more heating and transformative. They relate most to *samāna*, the fire element. *Samāna* means equalising. The *vinyāsa*, or movement, cultivates *prāṇa*, the air element: the *vinyāsa* always start with an inhalation, which most increases *prāṇa*. The finishing sequence, both inversions and sitting, and particularly headstand, deal with *udāna*, the ether element, and are expansive. However, each aspect of the practice contains all of the elements within it. Certain elements have a tendency to manifest more strongly with certain postures. This also depends on seasonal and climactic changes, phases of the moon and transitions of the planets. It is useful to note these changes and be aware of them as they occur and recur.

Figure 23.
The Five *Vāyu*.

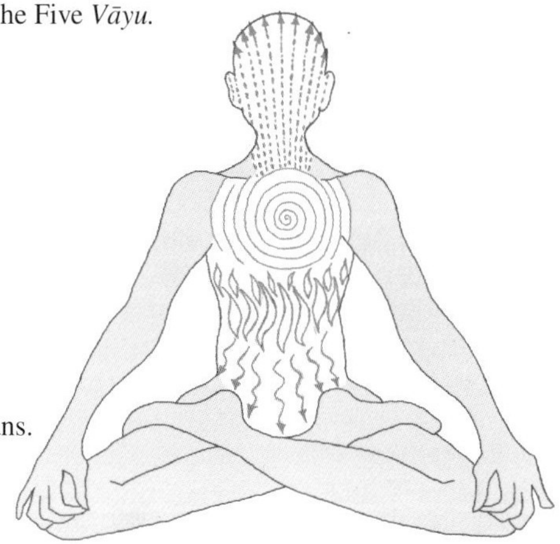

Udāna vāyu: **Ether**, Head region.
The sense organs, consciousness.

Prāṇa vāyu: **Air**, Chest region.
Inhalation, energy, absorption, vitality.

Samāna vāyu: **Fire**, Abdominal region.
The digestive organs, circulation.

Apāna vāyu: **Water**, Pelvic region.
Exhalation, elimination, reproductive organs.

Vyāna vāyu: **Earth**, Legs and Arms.
The skeleton, muscles and joints.

Yoga is a balance of opposing polarities: every body, every practice and every *āsana* is both accumulating (*prāṇa*) *and* eliminating (*apāna*), both contracted (*vyāna*) *and* expanded (*udāna*), involving body *and* mind. Balance these opposites by increasing awareness in each and every posture. For example, with forward bends the awareness is usually in the extremities, in the arms/shoulders (by binding the feet) and the legs/hamstrings. It is the mid section, both back and front that may need to be activated, the lower back extended and the internal organs the most contracted. With back bends it is more common to feel the contraction of the lower back rather than to feel the expansion of the front of the body; the latter is ideal. Overall the practice should harmonise and integrate all elements, not aggravate them.

The dominance of each of the *vāyu* in the body varies with each individual. This nature is exhibited as different body types, or constitutions, called the three *dośa*. They are *kapha*, *pitta* and *vāta*. *Kapha* combines both water and earth, *pitta* is governed by fire and water and *vāta* by air and ether. The *vāta* constitution is more mobile and is exhibited by a slender physical structure and nervous disposition. The *pitta* type is goal oriented, is exhibited by a more muscular, solid structure and assertive disposition. *Kapha* is more placid, is exhibited by a larger, weighty structure and a slower disposition. Every individual has a combination of all three *dośa*, with usually one or two of them pre-dominant. Depending on the individual's constitution, the practice can support or aggravate aspects of these *dośa*. That is, too much movement can support or aggravate *vāta* depending how extreme it is. Activity, focus and competitiveness can support or aggravate *pitta*, and no activity and quietness can support or aggravate *kapha*. The practice can be adjusted somewhat for each of these possibilities.

For example, the *vāta* type is attracted to *vinyāsa yoga*, and the *kapha* type tends to avoid physical exercise entirely. However, the attraction towards movement for the *vata* constitution is natural and healthy. It is over indulging this *dośa* in favour of supporting the qualities of the other two *dośa* that creates imbalance. For each individual always contains all three *dośa.* It is leaning too heavily on one type alone that is unbalanced. So slower movements will help support the *vāta* type. Doing a shorter practice tends to support the *kapha* type, and keeping the inner focus and *dristi* supports the *pitta* type.

The Three *Granthi*

> When the *Brahmā granthi* is pierced through... happiness is experienced in the vacuum of the heart... A *yogi's* body becomes divine, glowing, healthy, and emits a divine smell... In the second stage, the airs are united into one and begin moving in the middle channel... By this means the *Viṣṇu granthi* is pierced which is indicated by highest pleasure... Conquering then the pleasures of the mind, ecstacy is spontaneously produced which is devoid of evils, pains, old age, disease, hunger and sleep. When the *Rudra granthi* is pierced and the air enters the seat of the Lord then the perfect sound like that of a flute is produced. The union of the mind and the sound is called *rāja yoga*. The *yogi* becomes the creator and destroyer of the universe, like God.
>
> *HYP* 4: 69, 70, 71, 72, 74, 75, 76.

Each of the *granthi,* or knots, relates to the field of body, emotion and mind respectively. In most human beings each of these areas of the manifest Self has varying levels of disturbance, from illness, to addictions, to mild pain and anxiety. Hence the term "knot". When you are fully conscious of the *granthi*, when you have accepted and integrated the polarities in your life, you become untied. These knots are called *Brahmā granthi, Viṣṇu granthi* and *Śiva (Rudra) granthi*. i.e. the knot of the Creator, the knot of the Preserver and the knot of the Destroyer. *Brahmā, Viṣṇu* and *Śiva* are the three Gods, the *Trimūrti* of Hindu belief.

> *Granthis* represent blockages in man's awareness of himself at the different levels of consciousness; they obscure the true image of man's essential nature. Traditionally, *bandhas* were prescribed as one of the most effective means of untying these knots or blockages, existing as tension, anxieties, repressions and unresolved conflicts, thereby allowing us to rediscover our true nature.
>
> *Moola Bandha: the Master Key* p. 7

Figure 24: Brahmā the Creator

Brahma granthi is situated at the lowest *mūlādhāra chakra* and also governs the *svādhiṣṭhāna chakra*. This *granthi* deals with the most solid nature, bodily issues such as basic physical health, genetic history, physical liveliness, sexuality, pro-creation and the *kapha dośa*. It is concerned with the deepest desires and instincts.

The deity *Brahmā* is the Creator, bringing life out of the duality of light and dark, and represents the duality of existence (figure 24). *Brahmā* is the ultimate *guru*, which also means dark and light or *gu* and *ru*. *Brahmā* is the state of integration of these opposites. *Brahmā* is also represented in the term *haṭha, ha* meaning sun and *ṭha* meaning moon. *Haṭha yoga* is concerned with untying the *Brahmā granthi*: purifying and transcending issues relating to the physical body. It should be noted that each of the three *granthi* are intimately connected. No problem exists in isolation, an issue on one level will always affect an issue on another level. The more ingrained a problem, the more it affects the other levels.

Viṣṇu granthi is situated in the heart *chakra,* the *anāhata,* and governs the *maṇipūraka chakra* also. This *granthi* deals with both caring for the self and caring for others; the *maṇipūraka chakra* and heart *chakra* respectively. The *maṇipūraka* deals with survival: food, digestion, work, nourishing the self and the *pitta dośa*. The solar plexus *chakra* also governs many aspects of the nervous system. The *anāhata* deals with caring, relationship, connection and community. Eating disorders, unbalanced relationships and self isolation are common symptoms when the *Viṣṇu granthi* is disturbed.

The deity *Viṣṇu* is the Preserver or Balancer (figure 25). His area of governance is between the mind and body, balancing the emotional friction caused by the interaction of the two. Traditionally he is sent down to Earth to destroy the demons (illness, addictions, disorders etc) that have upset the balance. *Viṣṇu* embodies *śanti*: he offers unconditional love and healing ensues. The practice of *prāṇāyāma* is often prescribed to alleviate nervous system problems, the *nāḍī* (nerves) being intimately connected with the emotional field. As the nervous system becomes calmer, the *Viṣṇu granthi* becomes clearer. However, the *Viṣṇu granthi* is only fully untied when you have purified and transcended personal relationships - though you cannot have a relationship to anyone else beyond the relationship that you have to yourself. All of your external relationships mirror your internal ones. This tends to mean that when a man fully integrates his hidden female side (without sacrificing his masculinity) and when a woman fully integrates her hidden male side (without sacrificing her femininity) holism occurs.

Figure 25: Viṣṇu the Preserver

The *Śiva granthi* is situated at the third eye, the *ājñā chakra*, and also governs the throat *chakra, viśuddha*. This *granthi* deals with both thought and speech; the mind and its activities. An overactive or underactive intellect, disconnection from the physical body, becoming emotionally numb, continuous talking, or inability to communicate are common symptoms of this *granthi*. It is concerned with the *vāta dośa*.

> You talk when you cease to be at peace with your thoughts; and when you can no longer dwell in the solitude of your heart you live in your lips, and sound is a diversion and a pastime. And in much of your talking thinking is half murdered. For thought is a bird of space, that in a cage of words may indeed unfold its wings but cannot fly.
>
> *The Prophet*, p. 60.

Figure 26: Śiva the Destroyer

The deity *Śiva* is the Destroyer, he removes the old to make space for the new. (Figure 31). He represents the destroyer of the fixed mind-set, the breaker of bad habits. Through awareness of what is (self-acceptance) the mind becomes quiet and heightened perception takes its place. The practice of *rāja yoga,* or kingly meditation is said to untie the *Śiva granthi.* That is, purifying and transcending the mind. Complete lack of desire, the dissolution of the ego-mind, brings the isolated self back to universal self, to the highest *sahasrāra chakra.* Untying the *Śiva granthi* brings liberation, the gateway into true spiritual life where the mind and its functions become a willing public service to the higher awareness. Although the mind is the first and last obstacle to be surmounted, to suppress it rather than transcend it is undesirable. The former will only create more pressure. Complete transcendance is in the hands of God (*Śiva*).

Āsana, prāṇāyāma and meditation are each mentioned as aids to untying the *granthi.* In the *Aṣṭāṅga* practice this is typified in the expression *tristhānaṁ*, or three places of attention. They are posture, breathing and gaze. The postures begin to purify the lower *granthi* (body), *ujjāyi* breathing begins to purify the middle *granthi* (nervous system or emotion) and the withdrawal of the senses inherent in the *dṛiṣṭi* begins to purify the upper *granthi* (mind). From the perspective of the breath the inhalation brings life to the hidden areas of the body, blind spots and tensions stemming from the *granthi.* The exhalation releases tension, calming the mind. As the breath purifies, tensions release, the mind calms and the *granthi* begin to dissolve.

The three *bandha* are inextricably linked with the three *granthi.* As Śri T. Kriṣṇamacharya once said, the *bandha* are not something you do, but a blockage to be removed. In other words, the *granthi* and *bandha* are aspects of the same trio and the term lock or knot is synonymous. The term *bandha* on one level means the physical contraction of a specific part of the body to re-direct energy. That is, by holding the *āsana* in a centred way, the physical knots of the body untie. On a deeper level the *bandha* energy only becomes unlocked when the *granthi* are untied. It is stressed that awareness is crucial, that at this level the *bandha* are almost entirely psychological rather than physiological. That is, the physical practice of the *bandha* is very much secondary to self awareness and self acceptance and in some cases may hinder them.

The contraction of the *mūla bandha* is not a physical contraction at all. It is the raising of energy and awareness through the *mūlādhāra chakra* into the *suṣumṇā nāḍī.* In terms of the *granthi* this seems to imply the purification of the body, which certainly helps. More importantly, it is complete acceptance of the body *as it is.* This may appear paradoxical at first, but one condition does not prevent the other. It is acceptance that promotes true purification rather than the other way around.

When the body becomes capable of perfect stillness the *mūla bandha* becomes active and the *Brahmā granthi* is pierced through. The *uḍḍīyāna bandha* is the full movement of the diaphragm and is most associated with *prāṇāyāma* and the purification of the nervous system. The diaphragmatic movement tends to clear tension around the solar plexus, a common point for emotional blockage. At the most refined level this *bandha* is the raising of energy to the heart centre, transforming the bodily urges of survival into true caring and support. When the aggravated emotional body becomes transfigured by love, the *uḍḍīyāna* flies upward and the *Viṣṇu granthi* is pierced. The *jālandhara bandha* is not only the cessation of breath, but also the cessation of mental agitation. Despite the link to *prāṇāyāma*, this *bandha* is more closely tied to *pratyāhāra, dhāraṇā* and *dhyāna.* When the ego-mind surrenders to the divine emptiness the *Śiva granthi* is pierced.

The unlocking of the three *bandha* are a result of self development rather than self development being the result of the practice of the *bandha.* This is not to deny the practical nature of the *bandha:* applying them tends to increase awareness. However, the practice of these locks is not essential as far as self development is concerned. This may seem contrary to some traditional beliefs. Self development occurs through experiencing reality rather than desires, accomplishments and illusions.

True change is made possible when you are in contact with what is, when you realise what you are. It does not occur when you try to become something you are not. This is delusion. With the latter there can only be a constant war between the desire for what you should be and what you are. This is one of the more troubling truths that most *yoga* practitioners have to deal with. No amount of *āsana* or *prāṇāyāma* or meditation practice will make you a better person or hasten your development. Nothing will. For there is nothing better than being what you are, right now. This is the only way the *bandha* are truly activated and the knots untied.

The practice can only bring you into yourself if it is done with awareness. Awareness is the only key ingredient, all other processes are secondary. Awareness must involve some kind of contact with what is, or it is illusory. The practice *helps* to maintain this contact with reality. It is important not to slide into the path of least resistance or to avoid what is difficult.

If you become aware of *and* fully committed to your inner life (whatever that may be at the time) meaningful change is possible. If there is some level of suppression of this true inner world, no matter how it opposes external or imposed beliefs, deeper change is not possible. It is important to take full responsibility for this inner world rather than using it as an externalised weapon or moral bludgeon.

The word transcendance is used above to indicate awareness, acceptance and integration rather than "climbing away from." Complete acceptance is not *tamasic* or withdrawn and apathetic. Neither is it *rajasic,* that is actively seeking to purify the body or mind. It is *sattvic,* the balanced state beyond duality. Transcendance also indicates surrender to a higher principle, or God. No matter what difficulty, disease or problem arises, the multiple layers of its existence should be understood and embraced. The difficulty has a benefit, somehow, a purpose for that time and place. Disease becomes transformed and absorbed into the greater quality of gratefulness. Acceptance brings with it a degree of purification but the disease may still remain. Everybody grows old and dies. By accessing the timeless here and now, the ageing process is slowed and the individual remains forever young at heart.

Yoga practice generally increases sensitivity. Without improved sensitivity awareness is not likely to develop. From the external perspective (friends, family etc) or the individual's own perspective this may tend to be viewed as "getting worse" rather than "getting better". That is, becoming *more* rather than less affected by what is occurring. Being sensitive should not result in an inability to cope, but the ability to ask for help, to share, and to help in return. However, the tendency for some isolation with increased sensitivity is not only common but necessary. Self-support comes in various forms.

As you become more sensitive you will become increasingly aware of the different stages of contact and withdrawal that you have with yourself and with the environment. You will begin to accept that both of these stages are important, needing equal emphasis. To attempt to maintain complete openness one hundred percent of the time, or to remain closed from all external influence is unhealthy and delusional-you will be holding yourself in resistance to what is. Both of these states are extreme polarities, whether they are perceived as strength or openness is irrelevant. An individual needs both strong boundaries *and* a well oiled gate to allow visitors (change) in.

The idea that *āsana* practice will eventually bring about a perfect state of health is problematic. *Āsana* practice may make you stronger or more flexible, but in some areas it might not. Some change will always be there, but the form that change takes is beyond your control. To keep hoping that the future will bring perfection or even a moment of happiness is a problem which only self acceptance can resolve.

What is *yoga*? What is spiritual? Practices such as *āsana*, *prāṇāyāma* and meditation may refine concentration and encourage self-awareness, but no technique, be it gross or subtle, is innately more spiritual than anything else is. Spirit is. It pervades everything, so there is no thing that is not spirit. If I do this thing, this method of practice or that method, does it make me a better person? What is the "I" that is not good enough, that seeks to become better by doing these things? There is a conflict, a separation of the "I" that thinks and the "I" that is. The only pre-requisite to re-discover the latter "I" is awareness. Every philosophical idea and every technique is a passing state. Every method of teaching on the planet is within the field of body, emotion and mind. Each has a time and a place and each one of them is potentially useful. Each is an exercise one uses and an aid to awareness. But like a cloak one wears, ultimately it is to be discarded. Self is within. *Hare tatsat*. I am that I am.

As you learn to stay in contact with the body as it is, no matter how uncomfortable, self acceptance begins to manifest. When the truth of the body is actually experienced, transformation occurs. Through *yoga* practices the body can be directly experienced as impermanent, feeling it as sensation, movement and mostly empty space. Likewise for the mind. Self is neither of these things. I have a body, I am not that. I have a mind, I am not that. I have emotions, I am not that. With the emotions however, there is a always an underlying basis of peace, tranquility and love. This is all that remains.

> Your joy is your sorrow unmasked. And the selfsame well from which your laughter arises was oftentimes filled with your tears. And how else can it be? The deeper that sorrow carves into your being, the more joy you can contain.
>
> *The Prophet*, p. 29.

The *Nāḍī* and *Kuṇḍalinī*

Stemming from and interwoven with the *chakra* are the many *nāḍī*, closely associated with the nervous system. There are reportedly seventy-two thousand *nāḍī*. Of these there are thirteen principle nerves, each relating to the traditional organs of the body. Three of these are considered of most importance: *iḍā*, *piṅgalā* and *suṣumṇā*. *Iḍā nāḍī* is the left nerve and means pale (blue) conduit, *piṅgalā nāḍī* is the right nerve and means reddish conduit.

Iḍā and *piṅgalā* are closely associated with the left and right sympathetic cords. That is, the sympathetic cord which is concerned with withdrawal and cooling the system and the para-sympathetic cord which is concerned with growth and heating the system. *Suṣumṇā nāḍī* is the central nerve (spinal cord) meaning penetrating conduit. It is *sattva*, the rhythm beyond duality.

In figure 22 the dark line represents *piṅgalā*, culminates in the right nostril, is upward, masculine energy, governs the right side of the body and is also called *sūrya* or sun *nāḍī*. The lighter grey line represents *iḍā* starting in the left nostril, is downward, feminine energy, governs the left side of the body and is also called *chandra* or moon *nāḍī*.

The three principle nerves are directly related to the three *guṇas*, or qualities that are manifested in every part of the physical world: *tamas*, meaning inertia, *rajas*, meaning activity, and *sattva* meaning rhythm. Every individual manifests the first two *guṇas* to some extent or other. The development of *sattva*, also defined as tranquility, requires balancing *rajas* and *tamas* into one.

The moon moves in *iḍā* and is cooling (nectar) and *tamas*. The sun moves in *piṅgalā* and is heating (poison) and *rajas*. It is said that when *suṣumṇā* becomes active the *yogi* becomes dead to the world, invisible. Then the *yogi's* real work begins. *Iḍā* and *piṅgalā* indicate time, past and future respectively, *suṣumṇā* is the destroyer of time. It is the present moment and it is timeless.

> The *sannyasin* balances within himself both the male and female energies. Complete unto himself he is whole and independent. Having attained an equilibrium of *iḍā* and *piṅgalā* he becomes the knower of the known. *Aum*.
>
> *Dancing with Śiva*, *Sloka* 118 p. 347.

It is the endeavour of *yoga* to unite *apāna* with *prāṇa*, to completely resolve all duality, all polarity. The literal meaning for *apāna* is not eaten or unintegrated. It is common for *prāṇa* to be seen as something good and *apāna* as something bad. *Prāṇa* is life, *apāna* is death. The acceptance of the so called bad aspects of Self, or *apāna*, encourages the yoking or union of opposites: life and death are one.

In terms of fully understanding this concept the idea that *apāna* is purely about physical elimination is limited. The physical improvement of digestion and elimination may occur but the term *apāna* is analogous to the individual's unintegrated personality. *Yoga* is acknowledging, accepting and integrating the dark side rather than its removal.

Kuṇḍalinī means she who is coiled and is considered to be the mother of the universe, the force beyond duality. She is the serpent *śakti*, the divine power. The awakening of *kuṇḍalinī* is a tireless and esoteric task. It is a difficult subject to grasp with the mind because its basic premise goes against the thinking principle: Self is beyond mind and matter, and no amount of thinking or doing arrives at the state of *yoga*. In grasping the concepts of *iḍā, piṅgalā* and *suṣumṇā*, however, some light may have been shed on this subject.

The process of integration is the start of the journey. The blockages within each *chakra*, stemming from each of the three *granthi*, are resolved when Self becomes integrated and *suṣumṇā* is enlivened. That is, when the individual starts to integrate the "uneaten" parts of Self, he or she becomes whole. The *āsana* practice is both a vehicle to bring health and liveliness to the body and a method by which one may become aware of these unintegrated parts.

> The awakened *kuṇḍalinī* that is taken up to *maṇipūraka chakra* may drop down again to *mūlādhāra*. It has to be raised again with effort. One should become perfectly desireless and should be full of *vairāgya* (detachment) before he attempts to awaken *kuṇḍalinī*... When it is awakened it hisses like a serpent beaten with a stick and enters the hole of *suṣumṇā*. When it travels from *chakra* to *chakra,* layer after layer of the mind becomes open and the *yogi* acquires various *siddhis*.
>
> *The Science of Pranayama,* p. 16.

Figure 27. The Cadaceus: medical symbol of healing.

In most mythologies the serpent/crocodile is a potent image. It is a message of ancient history, the serpent-like articulation of the spine, and our root genetic memory. The serpent is a creature of divine purpose, though it is cold blooded, dispassionate and somewhat alien.

The Cadaceus symbol portrays *iḍā, piṅgalā* (serpents) and *suṣumṇā* (winged staff) and the awakening of consciousness to the divine spirit (flame). Each knot of the twin serpents represent each of the three *granthi* i.e. 3 ½ coils of *kuṇḍalinī* - the half a coil indicating the transcendant state beyond the duality of the *granthi.*

You must face your inner being, with your lower nature completely revealed before realisation of your higher nature may occur. It is no small paradox. Complete surrender to the higher nature must occur before the individual can fully experience what it is. This blind surrender will occur only after all other avenues are explored by the lower nature. The premature awakening of *kuṇḍalinī* rises through *iḍā* or *piṅgalā* rather than through the centre, and aggravates the unresolved polarities. The serpent requires the resolution of past and future before it can truly awaken. The surrender of the lower nature to the higher one is a struggle that should not be taken lightly. It occurs when it may and not through the ego's choosing.

The articulation of the spine is a physical snake-like attribute that is directly related to the *yoga* practice. By moving the body and enlivening the spinal cord the energy of *iḍā, piṅgalā* and *suṣumṇā* are activated and integrated. Awareness, again, is the key. The awakening of the serpent goddess is an image relating to the flexing of the individual's spiritual spine. The dispassionate nature of the serpent *śakti* must be met before you can truly face yourself in the mirror. The following excerpt describes the difficulty of awakening *kuṇḍalinī śakti.*

> The terrible trial which precedes initiation into discipleship comes when the pilgrim stands face to face with his human selfhood in its starkest power, self which has sacrificed and devoured its children must slay self in this last dread struggle. Is it a matter for wonder that so many fail who rush untimely to this encounter wherein victory must be gained without aid, or encouragement from man, or master or god?
>
> *The Sayings of the Ancient One*, p. 84.

Through great striving the polarised ego-mind is made subservient to the infant spiritual ego. Or in other words, the conditioned self and the constructs of mind surrender to that most fearful snake, universal consciousness. The loss of Self to the awakened serpent goddess is a grave risk, not to be undertaken lightly. Like an unruly child, if the base desires are not made subservient the serpent hisses and bites, soon returning to sleep.

The beginning of this shedding (as per the snake's skin) is an attempt towards the "desire to be desire-less", the one desire that absorbs all other desires. It is the last desire or polarity before liberation, the one that "eats its children". This is the process of *vairāgya*, or detachment. Eventually all of one's energy must be focused towards this end. As stated above, all other desires will be experienced first, all avenues exhausted by the ego before this becomes possible. This process may take years and lifetimes to develop.

As stated previously, it is not the sole purpose of this book to focus on the physical aspect of the practice and how to get into the postures, but to pose some of the questions as to why. I have continually circled around some core concepts, namely awareness and self-acceptance. This is the remarkable possibility that each individual has to move towards wholeness, of integrating the conflicting levels of Self. These levels have generally been categorised into polarities, opposing pairs that lead to the possibility of a third, integrated pathway. The majority of these triangular terms are listed below.

Mind:	Inhalation, strength, masculine, inspiration, upward, focused, tense, future, sun, *Śiva, pūraka, rajas, piṅgalā, prāṇa.*
Body:	Exhalation, flexibility, feminine, elimination, downward, relaxed, lazy, past, moon, *Brahmā, rechaka, tamas, iḍā, apāna.*
Emotion:	Pause, balance, multi-sexual, stillness, centre, tranquil, empty, present, universe, *Viṣṇu, sthamba, sattva, suṣumṇā, yoni-mudrā.*

The Eight Limbs

The term *Aṣṭāṅga* (eight limbs) was first used by the sage Patañjāli, the writer of a treatise on *yoga sūtras*, over two thousand years ago. As Guruji once said of these *sūtras*, "Small words, but *big* in meaning." The study of these *sūtras* presupposes a great deal of prior learning, where it is understood what Patañjāli's "small words" mean. This form of *yoga* would have been taught by aural transmission, handed down directly from teacher to student. As there is no currently accepted unbroken lineage on which to base these teachings, Patañjāli's deeper intent can only be guessed at. The following material is intended as an overview, rather any definitive insight into this older aural tradition. The eight limbs proposed by Patañjāli are:

Yama: self-restraint,
Niyama: personal observances,
Āsana: seat or posture,
Prāṇāyāma: development of energy,
Pratyāhāra: withdrawal of the mind,
Dhāraṇā: concentration,
Dhyāna: meditation and
Samadhi: enlightenment.

Historically the form of Patañjāli's *yoga* has little to link it with modern *āsana* practice. Often called *rāja* (king) *yoga*, or *yoga* of the mind, Patañjāli's *sūtras* are an exposition of the functioning of the mind and are principally concerned with meditation. His commentaries on the actual practices of *āsana* and *prāṇāyāma* are sparse and seem to be an aid to meditation only. However, the endeavour of all *yoga* practice is the same, whether *rāja* "mind" *yoga* or *haṭha* "physical" *yoga*. That is, awareness and realisation of Self. The *Yoga Sūtras of Patañjāli* underlay all modern *yoga*.

The third and fourth limbs of Patañjāli, *āsana* and *prāṇāyāma*, are the common starting point with any physical *haṭha yoga*. However, it is with the evolution of the first two limbs of Patañjāli, self-restraint and personal observances, that inner awareness truly unfolds. This leads to *Īśvara praṇidhānani*, surrender to God.

> *Ahimsā*: non-violence, *satya*: truth, *asteya*: non-stealing, *brahmacharya*: chastity and *aparigraha*: non-greediness are the five pillars of *yama*.
>
> When non-violence in speech, thought and action is established, one's aggressive nature is relinquished and others abandon hostility in one's presence. When firmly established in the practice of truth, words become so potent that whatever one says comes to realisation. When abstention from stealing is established, one is trusted by others and everything is shared with him, however precious it might be. When the *yogi* is firmly established in continence and chastity, then knowledge, vigour and energy flow to him. Knowledge of past and future lives unfolds when one is free from greed for possessions.
>
> *The Yoga Sūtras of Patañjāli,* 2: 30, 35, 36, 37, 38, 39

The five components of *yama*, self restraint, are considered universal vows and are not confined to time or place. The *yamas* evolve as a result of the practice of self awareness. When fully committed to the inner process it becomes impossible to harm oneself and so harm others. It is not an external imposition of morality. The *yamas* are concerned principally with the individual's relationship to the external.

> *Śaucha*: cleanliness, *santoṣa*: contentment, *tapas*: self-discipline, *svādhyāya*: self study and *Īśvara praṇidhānani*: surrender to God are the five pillars of *niyama*.
>
> Cleanliness of body and mind develops disinterest in contact with others for gratification. Contentment of consciousness brings supreme happiness. Inner self discipline burns away impurities and kindles the sparks of divinity. Self study leads towards the realisation of God. Surrender to God brings perfection in *samadhi*.
>
> *YSP,* 2: 32, 40, 42, 43, 44, 45

The process of the five *niyama* indicates the journey from gross Self to refined Self, step by step to *samādhi*. It is something like a personal self-study course. One begins with cleanliness, progresses to contentment, through self-discipline, into self-study, right to the gateway of *Brahmā*. These steps are also in accord with the five sheaths of an individual and the elements of nature. The anatomical (earth); physiological (water); psychological (fire); intellectual (air) and spiritual (ether) layers. Complementary to the five *yama,* the five *niyama* are the individual's relationship to the internal.

> The seat (*āsana*) should have the dual qualities of steadiness (*sthira*) and lightness (*sukha*). These qualities can be achieved by observing the reactions of the breath and body. From there the individual's dualities cease to disturb. Upon perfect stillness of the seat the uncontrolled and disturbed movements of the breath reduce (*prāṇāyāma*). The internal and external fluctuations of breath become soft and subtle when the transition (*sthamba*) between each breath becomes increasingly measured. The breath may then transcend consciousness (the thinking mind).
>
> *YSP,* 2: 46, 47, 48, 49, 50, 51

Patañjāli does not describe *āsana* practice per se, the literal meaning for this word being "seat". His use of the word indicates simply sitting still, rather than the practice of various *yogāsana*. The qualities of *sthira* and *sukha* are universally applicable to all times, whether meditating, practicing *āsana* or generally in daily life.

The Sanskrit Patañjāli uses regarding the gap between breaths is *sthamba* rather than *kumbhaka*. This means transition or pause rather than retention or lock. It is an absence of doing, unlike the more common practices of *prāṇāyāma* that are taught. This also indicates a meditation practice rather than breathing exercises. That is, the refinement of one of the most universal polarities, the integration of the your inhalation and exhalation into holism or unity. The final aspect (*sūtra* 51) where the breath transcends consciousness is also called *kevala kumbhaka* (see over for more details.) This is a definite step towards *pratyāhāra* and is crucial for understanding Patañjāli's higher limbs.

> Withdrawing the senses, mind and consciousness from contact with external objects and then drawing them inwards is *pratyāhāra*.
>
> *YSP*, 2: 54

> On *pratyāhāra*, or restraining the mind, Gheraṇḍa said: by its knowledge all passions like lust etc, are destroyed. Let one bring the *chitta* (thinking principle) under his control by withdrawing it whenever it wanders away by the various objects of sight.
>
> *The Gheraṇḍa Saṁhita*, 4: 1, 2

Pratya means indrawing and *ahāra* means food, or anything external. That is bringing awareness away from the external and sense gratification, to the internal. There are three zones of awareness, namely the inner zone, the middle zone and the outer zone. The inner zone involves both physical and emotional sensation, anything within the field of the body. For example, bodily sensations such as heat or cold, or emotionally charged sensations which arise from pain or the electrical heat of excitement. The inner zone is an aspect of reality of which an individual can be certain. Despite the impermanence of their nature, these sensations are real (to the individual) and are not based on externalised judgement or guesswork. The more the individual is aware of these sensations and takes responsibility for this inner world, the less likely he or she is to be judgmental.

The outer zone is anything *not* Self: clouds, room, colour, sound, smell etc. That is, anything external to the individual. The middle zone is where the inner and outer zones overlap, how they interrelate. The middle zone is often called the "meaning making" zone. This is where the individual makes meaning from what is directly observable in the inner or outer zones. The middle zone is interpretive and often analytical. It is normal in most human beings to resist the inner zone (and to an extent the outer zone) and stay in the middle zone. It is here the mind does its best (and worst) work.

For example, a sensation in the body arises from the arch of the spine in a back bend (inner zone). The mind will typically label that sensation as good or bad (middle zone). Alternatively, in the outer zone a particular sight or sound or smell is experienced. A sensation will then arise in the body (inner zone) and also be labeled in some manner (middle zone). This labeling will often be at a level below normal consciousness. As awareness develops you can begin to witness your inner zone more completely and observe this process taking place: your unconscious habits become conscious.

The practice of *pratyāhāra* is an attempt to stay in the inner zone, to bring the *chitta*, the mind in contact with this inner world. This does not mean an avoidance of all external contact, or an abandonment of responsibility. The practice of *āsana* increases awareness of the body allowing direct use of *pratyāhāra*, or withdrawal of the mind to the inner zone. The cultivation of the *dṛiṣṭi* is useful for this. *Pratyāhāra* can be defined as embodied awareness rather than non-involvement or suppression. This usually takes years of experiential practice to develop, not only through *āsana* but also in meditation and most importantly in daily life. At every waking moment, the mind keeps some contact with the body's sensations, with what is occurring in the moment.

It is particularly important, and most difficult, to stay in contact with sensations that have a strong emotional charge. There is usually a tendency to either externalise such feelings and blame them on circumstance or another individual, or deny the feeling altogether. An increase in the ability to be embodied, or somatically aware, equals a decrease in judgmental behavior. As soon as you deny such sensations and withdraw from acknowledging *any* feelings, a suppression of Self and an increase in judgmental behaviour occurs.

Pratyāhāra is not avoidance or disconnection from feeling (i.e. the senses) but the detachment from the mind's judgement that arises from feeling. Feelings are always there, it is becoming aware of them that matters. This does not imply that your feelings should be indulged, in particular the sense-gratification associated with the outer zone. Observe and accept what is occurring in the inner zone and the mind will stay clear. By observing or witnessing the senses dispassionately they begin to have less impact.

All feelings have a (momentary) location in the body. If not, then either there is limited awareness at that time, or it is not a feeling and some type of judgement is taking place instead. Part of this practice is to observe the location of each emotion, where it is in the body. Otherwise the emotion stays somewhat divorced from experience and unintegrated. One of the most useful times to practice this awareness is when you are talking, or waiting for your turn to talk. Try to keep part of your awareness within the field of your body rather than completely wrapped up in the imaginative drama of the middle zone. Improved concentration will be necessary.

> Fixing the consciousness on one point is concentration (*dhāraṇā*).
>
> *YSP*, 3: 1

Prolonged concentration is not possible without some withdrawal of the mind. There is always some distraction or other. The practice of *āsana* in conjunction with increased awareness leads to *pratyāhāra*. Essentially the practice of *pratyāhāra is* the practice of *vairāgya*. Withdrawal is not possible without *vairāgya* and true detachment is not tested without some difficulty e.g. the *āsana* practice. For instance, it is easy enough to be detached when a posture feels pleasant, but when it is uncomfortable, that is the true measure. The *āsana* practice is a mirror for life: ups and downs, pleasantness and unpleasantness. Unfortunately the deeper process of *yoga* goes out the window when one is driven by the desire to get to the next posture (or the next anything).

> Consistent practice (*abhyāsa*) and detachment (*vairāgya*) are the means to still the movements of consciousness.
>
> *YSP*, 1: 12

Although detachment suggests being unaffected or removed it may be more useful to say "to be open". That is, accepting of what is, open to what is. Even this phrase may be a little troublesome. It does not imply complete passivity or inaction. The concept of detachment may become an avoidance of what is, a lack of acceptance of reality.

> A steady continuous flow of attention is meditation (*dhyana*).
>
> *YSP, 3: 2*

Unfiltered observation is awareness without judgement. Unlike *dhāraṇā*, *dhyāna* meditation denotes a loss of control, the loss of the ego-self through inner zone awareness. This is only possible when the *vairāgya* (detachment) remains steady. Just as there are many different *āsana* methods, there are many methods of meditation. Each has its benefit. The emphasis on movement and the physical body in the *vinyāsa* system does not allow a great deal of stillness. Meditating (sitting) regularly counterbalances this. *Āsana* practice should lead towards some form of silent meditation or inner contemplation. Meditation can be done at any time of the day. It is useful to have a specific time for it, however, to minimise interruptions and distractions. Practice the following two methods:

1. *Kevala kumbhaka*. Sit upright in a comfortable (cross-legged) posture with the eyes closed. Begin by observing the breath. Do not try to restrain or control it in any way. Just observe. There will be two tendencies: either the mind will wander away from this passive awareness and drift into a thought or fantasy, or it will attempt to control the breath. Do neither. Just observe the breath. A cycle will develop between attention, inattention and control. As the ability to observe increases, inattention and control decrease. Slowly the breath will become more and more soft and subtle. Both the inhalation and exhalation will become neutralised as the *sthamba*, or pause, increases. Eventually the breath will simply become absent.

While the breath is absent, the mind will tend to be tranquil also. At some point (seconds or minutes later) the system will naturally re-assert itself and one will begin breathing again. There should be no strain or imposition while the breath is absent. The length of time this natural retention maintains itself will organically increase with more practice. This is the most refined *kumbhaka*, called *kevala* or alone. When the breath is absent, what is left? *Kevala* is the only *kumbhaka* that is an absence of doing. As far as *kevala kumbhaka* is concerned it does not matter whether your breath is capable of being deep or not. If you sit still for long enough the breathing becomes shallow regardless. As this stillness increases, awareness of the body's subtle movements of *prāṇa*, or energetic sensations tends to increase.

If the body's movement is more gross this awareness tends to decrease. Holding still in a posture allows greater awareness of this type and the *vinyāsa* generally does not. The *vinyāsa* purifies and brings life to the weaker aspects of the constitution. Through the movement, the life force that charges the *nāḍīs* increases. Without movement the life force generally stays at a minimum ebb. However, it is not until real stillness is maintained that awareness of the subtle Self is made. *Vinyāsa* and stillness go hand in hand.

2. *Rāja kevala kumbhaka*. In the same way you watch the breath, calmly watch the mind. Observe any thought that arises. As with the breath, the tendency is to become inattentive and unconsciously wander into fantasy, to run away with your thoughts. Take a mental step back and simply observe whichever thought is there. As you sits for longer periods, the mind begins to quiet, the various thoughts have less impact. *Vairāgya* is cultivated.

Eventually your thoughts become absent; awareness without analysis. The middle zone disappears and the inner and outer zone become one. As you get used to sitting still for longer and longer, the *chitta* will stay absent for longer and longer. When the mind is absent, what is it that perceives? Simply by sitting, sooner or later the mind and breath will become quiet.

Any technique, even the processes described above, are impositions. Whatever the activity of the mind or body, if you completely integrate your experience, then meaningful change will arise. Simply walking down the street and fully integrating that experience is *yoga*. Doing your *āsana* practice and yearning for change or the next posture is not. Sitting still (or any *yoga* technique) increases the capacity for awareness and integration. However, as the individual develops continual contact with the inner reality, the reliance on these techniques should slowly decrease rather than increase. That is, the mind can be quiet regardless of the activity.

> *Yogas chitta vṛtti nirodhaḥ.*
> *Yoga* is the cessation of the fluctuations of mind.
>
> *YSP*, 1: 2

The second *sūtra* of Patañjāli is probably the most well known: when the analytical mind becomes absent, there is only awareness. There are various levels of this experience, beginning with the bracketing of the judgemental mind in the meditation processes described above. This (one assumes) leads to the stage of "absorption *samādhi*".

> When the object of meditation engulfs the meditator, appearing as subject, self awareness is lost, this is *samādhi*.
>
> *YSP*, 3: 3

That is, the observation of "what is" engulfs consciousness. In the regular *Aṣṭāṅga* practice *pratyāhāra* can be cultivated, and therefore *vairāgya*. The practice of *pratyāhāra* leads to the higher limbs of Patañjāli: *dhāraṇā* (concentration), *dhyāna* (meditation) and *samādhi* (absorption in self). By directing the breath, *bandha* and *driṣti*, *dhāraṇā* is cultivated. Through observing the breath and observing the mind, as it is, *dhyāna* is cultivated. *Samādhi* may then arise, or not, as may be. The attainment of the state of *yoga* occurs through effortlessness and the grace of *Brahmā*.

Figure 28: Depiction of Patañjāli, also considered to be an incarnation of *Viṣṇu*.

This concludes the *yoga* philosophy section. Remember to keep your sense of humour. Do not take the practice, or yourself too seriously. Take what you will from every book or teacher that you encounter, but try to keep a light-hearted attitude. The practice may be the vehicle that guides your process, but it is the process that is important.

> The *yogi* should practice *haṭha yoga* in a small room, situated in a solitary place, being four cubits square, and free from stones, fire, water, disturbances of all kinds, and in a country where justice is properly administrated, where good people live, and food can be obtained easily and plentifully... Having seated in such a room and free from all anxieties, he should practice *yoga*, as instructed by his *Guru*.
>
> *HYP*, 1: 12, 14

How to Use this Book

This book is intended as a guide to the traditional practice of *Aṣṭāṅga yoga*. However, it cannot replace instruction from an experienced teacher. The photographic *vinyāsa* section of this book (from page 52) has kept to the traditional and/or most common variations of the movements between *āsana*. Each line of this section either starts and finishes with *Samasthitiḥ* or downward dog. The breath indicated for the latter is usually followed or preceded by ellipses (e.g. Exhale...) This is to show both the continuation of the *vinyāsa* to the next line (or from the previous line) and also the option of coming back to *Samasthitiḥ* after downward dog for full *vinyāsa*. (See figure 29).

Figure 29.

From *Krounchāsana* ☞ Exhale Inhale **Exhale...**

...Exhale + Inhale Exhale Inhale + 5 Breaths

Figure 30.
Full *vinyāsa* into *Śalabhāsana*.

Ex. In. Ex. In. Exhale In. + 5 Br. Ex. + 5 Br. Inhale Exhale

An example where full *vinyāsa* is recommended, but not shown in the photographic *vinyāsa* section, is *Śalabhāsana*, the locust posture (figure 30). This *vinyāsa* is different from other full *vinyāsa* as you come into the posture before doing upward and downward dog. This is applied to most postures where you lie on your belly.

Ellipses are also used to indicate the ideal breath (figure 31). This is often a single inhalation from downward dog to jump into a posture, even if it is more common to take three or four breaths. For example, jumping into most forward bends on a single inhalation is often difficult, so when learning take more breaths as necessary. As you becomes familiar with the sequence the number of breaths between *āsana* will ideally reduce until it is only one breath from downward dog into most postures, or the single inhalation to jump through and bind the hands (inhale head up) in the case of forward bends. The *vinyāsa* section of this book details the optimum movements and breaths.

If you have an injury, the reverse should be applied: more breaths to come into a posture (if the posture is possible at all) and hence greater awareness to facilitate the healing process. As the area heals, then once more minimise the breaths into and out of each *āsana*. Be aware of any extra breaths taken and move the body accordingly, in time with the breath. This avoids the tendency to become floppy physically or mentally when not sticking to the correct *vinyāsa*. There should be no sense of hurrying when trying to minimise the number of breaths between *āsana*. No matter how quick the movement, the breathing remains stable.

Figure 31.

Exhale **Inhale...** Inhale Exhale + 5 Breaths

Figure 32.

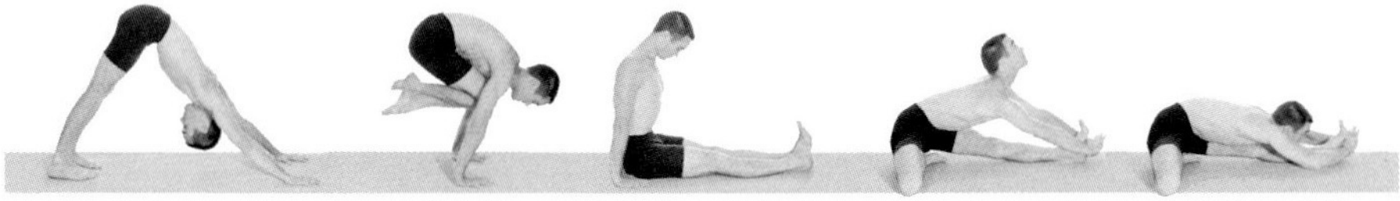

Exhale Inhale ...Inhale + Exhale... ...Exhale + Inhale Exhale + 5 Br.

Figure 32 shows the more common breathing pattern with forward bends: jump into *Daṇḍāsana* on the inhalation. When the exhalation starts, move into the appropriate posture and bind the front foot. Inhale and bring the head up, lengthening the spine. Exhale into the complete posture. The extra breath facilitates ease with the movements and is slower and less intense. Even though it is not the "correct" *vinyāsa*, it is appropriate for most practitioners.

Figure 33.

Exhale + 5 Br. Inhale + Ex. Inhale... Inhale Exhale + 5 Br.
Vinyāsa (jump back)

To avoid redundancy the *vinyāsa* between sides of the same postures have usually been indicated by the phrase "**Vinyāsa** (jump back)", rather than picturing the same *vinyāsa* for each side of every *āsana*. (Figure 33). The process of the learning *vinyāsa*, as indicated in figure 11 is the minimum standard. i.e. jump back every second side. Half *vinyāsa* is considered optimum (jump back both sides) and full *vinyāsa* for occasional practice.

AṢṬĀṄGA YOGA MANTRA

OM

vande gurūṇam charaṇāra vinde
sandarśita svātma sukhāve bodhe
niḥśreyase jāṇgalikāyamāne
saṁsāra hālāhala mohaśantyai

ābāhu puruṣakāraṁ
śaṅkachakrāsi dhāriṇam
sahasra śirasam śvetuṁ
prāṇamāmi patañjālim

OM

I pray to the lotus feet of the supreme Guru,
who teaches the good knowledge, showing the way
to knowing the self-awakening great happiness,
who is the doctor of the jungle, able to remove
the poison of the ignorance of conditioned existence.

In his guise as the divine serpent,
with 1000 white radiant heads,
human in form down to the shoulders,
holding the sword of discrimination,
the fire-wheel of time,
and the conch of divine sound,
to the sage Patañjāli I prostrate.

SŪRYANAMASKARA A x5

(0)	Inhale (1)	Exhale (2)	Inhale (3)	Exhale (4)	Inhale (5)	Exhale + 5 Breaths (6)	Inhale (7)	Exhale (8)	Inhale (9)	Exhale
Dṛiṣṭi:	3rd Eye	Nose	3rd Eye	Nose	3rd Eye	Nose	3rd Eye	Nose	3rd Eye	Nose
Samasthitiḥ	**Ūrdhva Vṛkṣāsana**	**Uttānāsana A**	**Uttānāsana B**	**Chaturāṅga Daṇḍāsana**	**Ūrdhva Mukha Śvānāsana**	**Adho Mukha Śvānāsana**	**Uttānāsana B**	**Uttānāsana A**	**Ūrdhva Vṛkṣāsana**	**Samasthitiḥ**

SŪRYANAMASKARA B x5

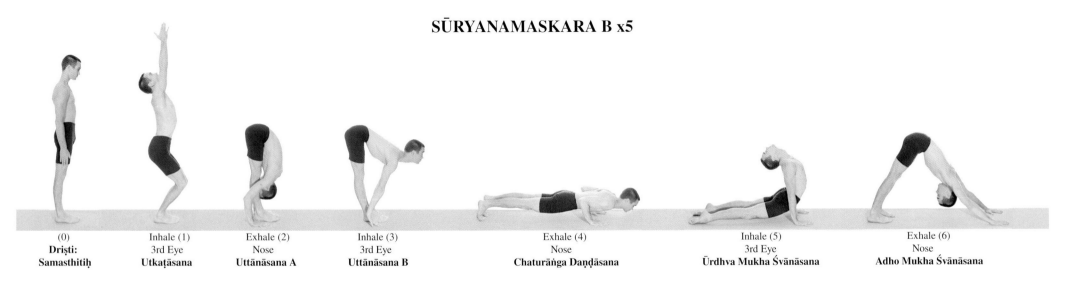

(0)	Inhale (1)	Exhale (2)	Inhale (3)	Exhale (4)	Inhale (5)	Exhale (6)
Dṛiṣṭi:	3rd Eye	Nose	3rd Eye	Nose	3rd Eye	Nose
Samasthitiḥ	**Utkaṭāsana**	**Uttānāsana A**	**Uttānāsana B**	**Chaturāṅga Daṇḍāsana**	**Ūrdhva Mukha Śvānāsana**	**Adho Mukha Śvānāsana**

Inhale (7)
3rd Eye
Vīrabhadrāsana A

Exhale (8)
Nose
Chaturāṅga Daṇḍāsana

Inhale (9)
3rd Eye
Ūrdhva Mukha Śvānāsana

Exhale (10)
Nose
Adho Mukha Śvānāsana

Inhale (11)
3rd Eye
Vīrabhadrāsana A

Exhale (12)
Nose
Chaturāṅga Daṇḍāsana

Inhale (13)
3rd Eye
Ūrdhva Mukha Śvānāsana

Exhale + 5 Breaths (14)
Nose
Adho Mukha Śvānāsana

Inhale (15)
3rd Eye
Uttānāsana B

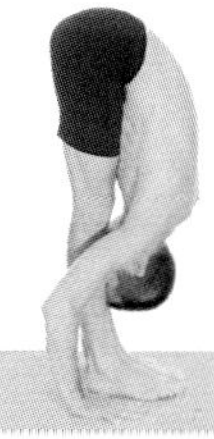

Exhale (16)
Nose
Uttānāsana A

Inhale (17)
3rd Eye
Utkaṭāsana

Exhale (0)
Nose
Samasthitiḥ

STANDING ĀSANA

Dṛiṣṭi: Nose
Hasta Pādāṅguṣṭhāsana & Pāda Hastāsana

Hand
Utthita Tri Koṇāsana

Hand
Utthita Tri Koṇāsana

Hand
Parivṛtta Tri Koṇāsana

Hand
Parivṛtta Tri Koṇāsana

Hand
Utthita Pārśva Koṇāsana

Hand
Utthita Pārśva Koṇāsana

Hand
Parivṛtta Pārśva Koṇāsana

Hand
Parivṛtta Pārśva Koṇāsana

Nose

Nose
B

Nose
C

Nose
D

Nose
Utthita Pārśvottānāsana

Nose
Utthita Pārśvottānāsana

Foot
Utthita Hasta Pādāṅguṣṭhāsana

Side
Utthita Pārśvasahita

Nose
Utthita Eka Pādāsana

Foot
Utthita Hasta Pādāṅguṣṭhāsana

Side
Utthita Pārśvasahita

Nose
Utthita Eka Pādāsana

Nose
Ardha Baddha Padmottānāsana

Hand
Utkaṭāsana

Hand
Vīrabhadrāsana A

Hand
Vīrabhadrāsana A

Hand
Vīrabhadrāsana B

Hand
Vīrabhadrāsana B

PRIMARY ĀSANA

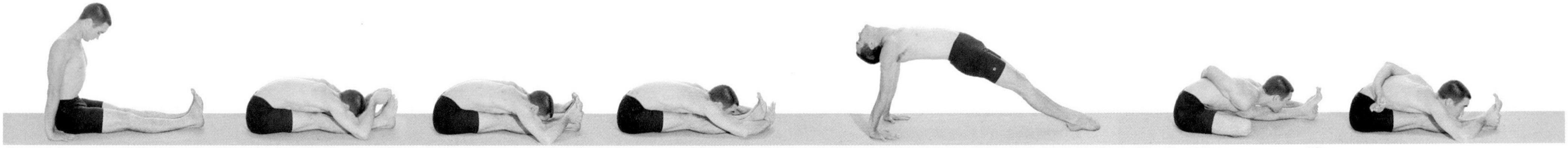

Nose **Daṇḍāsana**

Nose **Paśchimottānāsana A**

Nose or Foot **B**

Foot **C**

Nose **Pūrvottānāsana**

Nose **Ardha Baddha Padma Paśchimottānāsana**

Foot **Tirieng Mukha Eka Pāda Paśchimottānāsana**

Foot **Jānu Śīrṣāsana A**

Foot **Jānu Śīrṣāsana B**

Foot **Jānu Śīrṣāsana C**

Foot **Marīchyāsana A**

Nose **Marīchyāsana B**

Side **Marīchyāsana C**

Side **Marīchyāsana D**

Nose **Navāsana x5** ☞ · Nose **Lolāsana** · Nose **Bhuja Pīḍāsana** · 3rd Eye **Kūrmāsana** · Nose **Supta Kūrmāsana** · Nose **Garbha Piṇḍāsana** · Nose **Kukkuṭāsana**

Nose **Baddha Koṇāsana A** · Nose **B** · Nose **C** · Nose **Upaviṣṭha** · Upward **Koṇāsana A & B** · Navel **Supta Koṇāsana** · Foot **Supta Hasta Pādāṅguṣṭhāsana** · Side **Supta Pārśvasahita**

Foot **Supta Hasta Pādāṅguṣṭhāsana** · Side **Supta Pārśvasahita** · Upward **Ubbaya Pādāṅguṣṭhāsana** · Nose or Feet **Ūrdhva Mukha Paśchimottānāsana** · Nose **Setu Bandhāsana**

INTERMEDIATE ĀSANA

Side **Pāśāsana** | Foot **Krounchāsana** | Nose **Śalabhāsana A** | Nose **Śalabhāsana B** | Nose **Bhekāsana**

Nose **Dhanurāsana** | Nose **Pārśva Dhanurāsana** ☞ | Nose **Dhanurāsana** | Nose **Uṣṭrāsana** | Nose **Laghu Vajrāsana** | Nose **Kapotāsana A** | Nose **Kapotāsana B**

Nose **Supta Vajrāsana** | Nose **Up & down x5** | Nose **+ 5 Breaths** | Nose **Bakāsana A** | Nose **Bakāsana B** (Jump) | Side **Bharadvajāsana**

Side **Ardha Matsyendrāsana** | Foot **Eka Pāda Śīrṣāsana** | Nose **Dwi Pāda Śīrṣāsana** | 3rd Eye **Yoga Nidrāsana** | Nose **Tittibhāsana A** | Nose **B** (+ walk) | Nose **C**

Nose
Pincha Mayūrāsana

Nose
Karandavāsana

Nose
Mayūrāsana

Nose
Nakrāsana

Upward
Vātāyanāsana

Upward
Parighāsana

Nose Upward
Gomukhāsana A & B

Nose Upward
Gomukhāsana A & B

Nose Side
Supta Ūrdhva Pāda Vajrāsana

Nose Side
Supta Ūrdhva Pāda Vajrāsana

Nose
Mukta Hasta Śīrṣāsana A

B

C

Nose
Baddha Hasta Śīrṣāsana A

B

C

D

ADVANCED A ĀSANA

Foot **Vasiṣṭhāsana**

Hand **Viśwāmitrāsana**

3rd Eye **Kaśyapāsana**

Foot **Chakorāsana**

Hand **Bhairavāsana**

Nose **Skandāsana**

Upward **Dūrvāsāsana**

Nose **Ūrdhva Kukkuṭāsana A**

Nose **Ūrdhva Kukkuṭāsana B**

Nose **Ūrdhva Kukkuṭāsana C**

Nose **Gālavāsana**

Nose **Eka Pāda Bakāsana A**

Nose **Eka Pāda Bakāsana B**

Nose **Kouṇḍinyāsana A**

Nose **Kouṇḍinyāsana B**

Nose **Aṣṭāvakrāsana A**

Nose **Aṣṭāvakrāsana B**

Nose **Aṣṭāvakrāsana B**

Side **Pūrṇa Matsyendrāsana**

Nose Upward Nose Nose Upward Nose Nose Foot Side Nose Foot Side

Viranchyāsana A **Viranchyāsana A** **Viranchyāsana B** **Viranchyāsana B**

Nose
Viparīta Daṇḍāsana

Nose
Eka Pāda Viparīta Daṇḍāsana

Nose
Viparīta Śalabhāsana

Nose
Gaṇḍa Bheruṇḍāsana

Foot
Hanumānāsana

Nose
Supta Trivikramāsana

Hand
Dīghāsana A

Nose
Dīghāsana B

Hand
Dīghāsana A

Nose
Dīghāsana B

Nose
Trivikramāsana

Hand
Naṭarājāsana

Nose
Rāja Kapotāsana

Nose
Eka Pāda Rāja Kapotāsana

ADVANCED B ĀSANA

Nose **Mūla Bandhāsana** | Nose **Nahuśāsana A** | Nose **B** | Nose **C** | Nose **Vṛśchikāsana A** | Nose **Śayanāsana** | Nose **Buddhāsana**

Foot **Kapilāsana** | Foot **Ākarṇa Dhanurāsana A** | Upward **B** | Foot **Ākarṇa Dhanurāsana A** | Upward **B**

Nose **Pādāṅguṣṭha Dhanurāsana A** | Nose **B** | Nose **A** | Nose **Marīchyāsana E** | Side **Marīchyāsana F** | Nose **Marīchyāsana G**

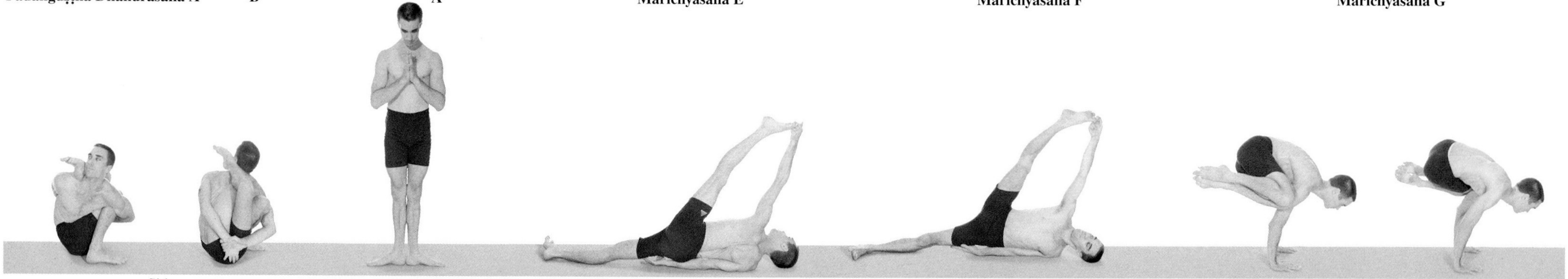

Side **Marīchyāsana H** | Nose **Tāḍāsana** | Foot **Samānāsana** | Nose **Pārśva Bakāsana**

Nose
Puṇga Kukkuṭāsana

Nose
Eka Pāda Dhanurāsana

Nose
Eka Pāda Kapotāsana

Nose
Paryāṅgāsana A

Nose
B

Nose
Parivṛttāsana A

Nose
Parivṛttāsana B

Nose
Yoni Daṇḍāsana

Hand
Yoga Daṇḍāsana

Nose
Bhuja Daṇḍāsana

Nose
Pārśva Daṇḍāsana

Nose
Ūrdhva Daṇḍāsana B

Nose
Adho Daṇḍāsana

Nose
Sama Koṇāsana

Nose
Omkarāsana

BACK BENDING
ĀSANA & VINYĀSA

Inhale + 5 Breaths
Ūrdhva Dhanurāsana
Dṛiṣṭi: Nose (for all the following)

Exhale

Inhale + 5 Breaths

Exhale

Inhale + 5 Breaths + Exhale

Inhale

Inhale

Inhale

Inhale
Drop Back x5 (Primary level)

Exhale

Exhale

Exhale

Inhale

Inhale

Inhale...

...Exhale
Handstand drop-over x5 (Intermediate level)

Inhale

Inhale
(+ 5 Breaths first time only)
Vṛkṣāsana

Exhale

Exhale

Inhale

Inhale

Inhale...

...Exhale | Inhale | Inhale | Exhale | Exhale | Inhale | Inhale | Exhale | Exhale...

Viparīta Chakrāsana x 5 (Advanced level)

...Exhale | Inhale | Inhale | Exhale + 5 Breaths + Inhale | Exhale | Inhale | Inhale | Inhale

Final Drop-over ☞

Vṛśchikāsana B

Inhale
Final Back Bending (all)

Exhale + 5 Breaths
Setu Bandhāsana

Inhale
Up & down x5

Exhale

Exhale + 5 Breaths
Chakra Bandhāsana

Exhale + 10 Breaths
Paśchimottānāsana

FINISHING SEQUENCE
ĀSANA & VINYĀSA

Inhale

Exhale (4)

Inhale (5)

Exhale (6)

Inhale (7)

Exhale + 10 Breaths

Inhale + 25 Breaths (8)
Navel
Sālamba Sarvāṅgāsana

Exhale + 10 Breaths + Inhale (8)
Navel
Halāsana

Exhale + 10 Breaths (8)
Navel
Karṇa Pīḍāsana

Inhale + 10 Breaths (8)
Navel
Ūrdhva Padmāsana

Exhale + 10 Breaths + In. (8)
Navel
Piṇḍāsana

Exhale + 10 Breaths + In. (8)
Nose
Matsyāsana

Exhale + 10 Breaths (8)
Nose
Uttāna Pādāsana

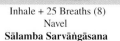

Inhale
Chakrāsana

Exhale (9)

Inhale (10)

Exhale (11/6)

Inhale (7)

Exhale

Inhale + 25 Breaths (8)
Nose
Śīrṣāsana

Exhale + 10 Breaths (9)
Nose
Ūrdhva Daṇḍāsana A

Inhale
Up & down x5 ☞

Exhale

Exhale + 10 Breaths
Eyes closed
Balāsana

Inhale

Exhale (4)

Inhale (5)

Exhale (6)

Inhale (7)

Exhale + 10 Breaths (8)
Nose
Baddha Padmāsana

Exhale + 10 Breaths (9)
3rd Eye
Yoga Mudrā

Exhale + 25 Breaths (10)
Nose
Padmāsana/Jñāna Mudrā

Inhale + 25 Breaths (11)
Nose
Utpluthiḥ

Exhale (12)

Inhale (13)

Exhale (14)
(do full vinyāsa for the mangala mantra)

Inhale

Take rest

STANDING VINYĀSA

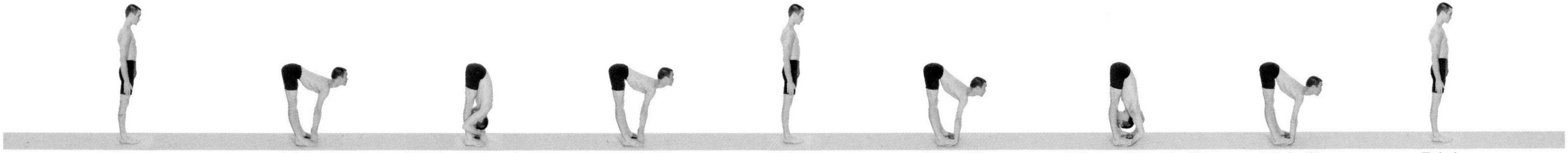

...Exhale   Inhale (1)   Exhale + 5 Breaths (2)   Inhale (3)   Exhale   Inhale (1)   Exhale + 5 Breaths (2)   Inhale (3)   Exhale...

Samasthitiḥ   **Hasta Pādāṅguṣṭhāsana**   **Pāda Hastāsana**

...Exhale   Inhale (1)   Exhale + 5 Breaths (2)   Inhale (3)   Exhale + 5 Breaths (4)   Inhale (5)   Exhale + 5 Breaths (6)   Inhale (7)   Exhale + 5 Breaths (8)   Inhale (9)   Exhale...

Utthita Tri Koṇāsana   **Utthita Tri Koṇāsana**   **Parivrtta Tri Koṇāsana**   **Parivṛtta Tri Koṇāsana**

...Exhale   Inhale (1)   Exhale + 5 Breaths (2)   Inhale (3)   Exhale + 5 Breaths (4)   Inhale (5)   Exhale + 5 Breaths (6)   Inhale (7)   Exhale + 5 Breaths (8)   Inhale (9)   Exhale...

Utthita Pārśva Koṇāsana   **Utthita Pārśva Koṇāsana**   **Parivṛtta Pārśva Koṇāsana**   **Parivṛtta Pārśva Koṇāsana**

...Exhale Inhale (1) Exhale + Inhale (2) Exhale (3) Inhale + Exhale (4) Inhale + Exhale (5) Inhale (1) Exhale + Inhale (2) Ex. + 5 Breaths (3) Inhale + Exhale (4) Inhale (5 & 1) Exhale + Inhale (2) Ex. + 5 Br. (3)

Prasārita Pādottānāsana A   **Prasārita Pādottānāsana B**   **Prasārita Pādottānāsana C**

Inhale + Exhale (4) (5 = arms wide full vinyāsa only) Inhale (1) Exhale + Inhale (2) Ex. + 5 Breaths (3) Inhale + Exhale (4) Inhale (5) Exhale Inhale (1) Exhale + 5 Breaths (2) Inhale (3) Exhale + 5 Breaths (4) Inhale (5) Exhale...

Prasārita Pādottānāsana D **Utthita Pārśvottānāsana** **Utthita Pārśvottānāsana**

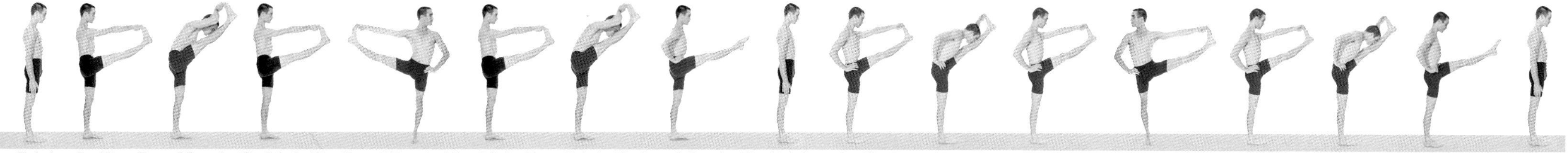

...Exhale In. (1) Ex. + 5 Breaths (2) Inhale (3) Ex. + 5 Breaths (4) Inhale (5) Exhale (6) In. + 5 Breaths (7) Exhale In. (8) Ex. + 5 Breaths (9) Inhale (10) Ex. + 5 Breaths (11) Inhale (12) Ex. (13) In. + 5 Br. (14) Exhale...

Utthita Hasta Pādāṅguṣṭhāsana **Utthita Pārśvasahita** **Utthita Eka Pādāsana** **Utthita Hasta Pādāṅguṣṭhāsana** **Utthita Pārśvasahita** **Utthita Eka Pādāsana**

...Exhale In. (1) Ex. + 5 Br. (2) In. + Ex. (3) In. (4) Exhale In. (5) Ex. + 5 Br. (6) In. + Ex. (7) In. (8) Exhale In. (1) Ex. (2) In. (3) Exhale (4) Inhale (5) Exhale (6) In... + 5 Br. + Ex. (7) Inhale (8)

Ardha Baddha Padmottānāsana **Ardha Baddha Padmottānāsana** **Utkaṭāsana**

Exhale (9/4) Inhale (5) Exhale (6) In. + 5 Breaths (7) Ex. + 5 Breaths (8) In. + 5 Breaths (9) Ex. + 5 Breaths (10) Inhale - up (11) Exhale (12) Inhale (13) Exhale (14)

Vīrabhadrāsana A **Vīrabhadrāsana B**

PRIMARY VINYĀSA

...Exhale (6) | Inhale... | In. + 5 Breaths + Ex. (7) **Dandāsana** | Inhale (8) | Exhale + 5 Breaths (9) **Paśchimottānāsana A** | Inhale (8) | Exhale + 5 Breaths (9) **Paśchimottānāsana B** | Inhale (8) | Exhale + 5 Breaths (9) **Paśchimottānāsana C** | Inhale + Exhale (10) | Inhale (11) (jump back optional)

Exhale (12) | Inhale (13) | Exhale (14/6) | Inhale... | Inhale + Exhale (7) | Inhale + 5 Breaths (8) **Pūrvottānāsana** | Exhale (9) | Inhale (10) | Exhale (11) | Inhale (12) | Exhale (13)...

...Exhale (6) | Inhale... | Inhale (7) | Ex. + 5 Br. (8) | In. + Ex. (9) **Ardha Baddha Padma Paśchimottānāsana** | Inhale (10)... **Vinyāsa** (jump back) | Inhale (14) | Ex. + 5 Br. (15) | In. + Ex. (16) **Ardha Baddha Padma Paśchimottānāsana** | Inhale (17) | Exhale (18) | Inhale (19) | Exhale (20)...

...Exhale (6) | Inhale... | Inhale (7) | Ex. + 5 Br. (8) | In. + Ex. (9) **Tirieng Mukha Eka Pāda Paśchimottānāsana** | Inhale (10)... **Vinyāsa** (jump back) | Inhale (14) | Ex. + 5 Br. (15) | In. + Ex. (16) **Tirieng Mukha Eka Pāda Paśchimottānāsana** | Inhale (17) | Exhale (18) | Inhale (19) | Exhale (20)...

...Exhale (6) | Inhale... | Inhale (7) | Exhale + 5 Br. (8) **Jānu Śīrṣāsana A** | In. + Ex. (9) | Inhale (10)... **Vinyāsa** (jump back) | Inhale (14) | Ex. + 5 Br.(15) **Jānu Śīrṣāsana A** | In. + Ex. (16) | Inhale (17) | Exhale (18) | Inhale (19) | Exhale (20)...

...Exhale (6) Inhale... Inhale (7) Exhale + 5 Br. (8) In. + Ex. (9) Inhale (10)... Inhale (14) Ex. + 5 Br. (15) In. + Ex. (16) Inhale (17) Exhale (18) Inhale (19) Exhale (20)...

Jānu Śīrṣāsana B **Vinyāsa** (jump back) **Jānu Śīrṣāsana B**

...Exhale (6) Inhale... Inhale (7) Exhale + 5 Br. (8) In. + Ex. (9) Inhale (10)... Inhale (14) Ex. + 5 Br. (15) In. + Ex. (16) Inhale (17) Exhale (18) Inhale (19) Exhale (20)...

Jānu Śīrṣāsana C **Vinyāsa** (jump back) **Jānu Śīrṣāsana C**

...Exhale (6) Inhale... Inhale (7) Exhale + 5 Br. (8) In. + Ex. (9) Inhale (10)... Inhale (14) Ex. + 5 Br. (15) In. + Ex. (16) Inhale (17) Exhale (18) Inhale (19) Exhale (20)...

Marīchyāsana A **Vinyāsa** (jump back) **Marīchyāsana A**

...Exhale (6) Inhale... Inhale (7) Ex. + 5 Br. (8) In. + Ex. (9) Inhale (10)... Inhale (14) Ex. + 5 Br. (15) In. + Ex. (16) Inhale (17) Exhale (18) Inhale (19) Exhale (20)...

Marīchyāsana B **Vinyāsa** (jump back) **Marīchyāsana B**

...Exhale (6) Inhale... In. + 5 Br. + Ex. (7) Inhale (8) Exhale (9) Inhale (10) Exhale (11) Inhale... In. + 5 Br. + Ex. (12) Inhale (13) Exhale (14) Inhale (15) Exhale (16)...

Marīchyāsana C **Marīchyāsana C**

...Exhale (6) Inhale... In. + 5 Br. + Ex. (7) Inhale (8) Exhale (9) Inhale (10) Exhale (11) Inhale... In. + 5 Br. + Ex. (12) In. (13) Exhale (14) Inhale (15) Exhale (16)...

Marīchyāsana D **Marīchyāsana D**

...Exhale (6) | Inhale... | In. + 5 Br. + Ex. (7) **Navāsana** (3 - 5 times) | Inhale (8) **Lolāsana** | In. + 5 Br. + Ex. (7) **Navāsana** | Inhale (8) **Lolāsana** | In. + 5 Br. + Ex. (7) **Navāsana** | Inhale... (8) **Lolāsana** | Inhale... | Inhale | Exhale (9) | Inhale (10) | Exhale (11)...

...Exhale (6) | Inhale... | Inhale (7) | Exhale + 5 Br. (8) **Bhujapīḍāsana** | Inhale... | Inhale (9) | (Exhale) | Inhale (10) | Exhale (11) | Inhale (12) | Exhale (13)...

...Exhale (6) | Inhale... | In. + 5 Br. (7) **Kūrmāsana** | Ex. + 5 Br. (8) **Supta Kūrmāsana** | In. +Ex. (9) | Inhale (10) | (Exhale) | Inhale (11) | Exhale (12) | Inhale (13) | Exhale (14/6)

Inhale (7) | Ex. + 5 Br. (8) **Garbha Piṇḍāsana** | Inhale Rolling x 9 ☞ | Exhale | Inhale | Exhale | Inhale | Exhale | Inhale | Exhale | Inhale | Exhale | Inhale | Exhale | Inhale | Exhale | Inhale | Exhale | Inhale | Exhale | In. + 5 Br. (9) **Kukkuṭāsana**

Inhale (10) | Exhale (11) | Inhale (12) | Exhale (13/6) | Inhale... | In. (7) | Ex. + 5 Br. (8) **Baddha Koṇāsana A** | Ex. + 5 Br. (8) **B** (optional) | In. + 5 Br. (9) **C** | Inhale (10) | Exhale (11) | Inhale (12) | Exhale (13)...

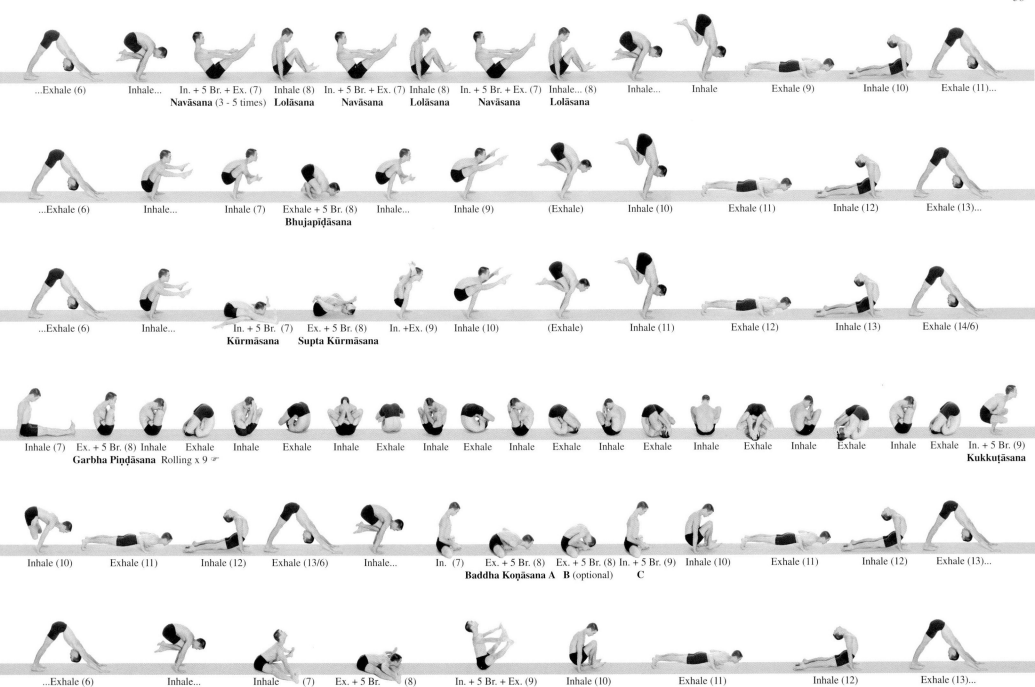

...Exhale (6) | Inhale... | Inhale (7) | Ex. + 5 Br. (8) **Upaviṣṭha Koṇāsana A** | In. + 5 Br. + Ex. (9) **B** | Inhale (10) | Exhale (11) | Inhale (12) | Exhale (13)...

...Exhale (6) Inhale... Inhale (7) Exhale In. + 5 Br. + Ex. (8) In. (9) (Exhale) In + Ex. (10) In. (11) Exhale (12) Inhale (13) Exhale (14)...

Supta Koṇāsana

...Exhale (6) Inhale... Inhale (7) Exhale Inhale (8) Exhale + 5 Breaths (9) Inhale (10) Ex. + 5 Br. (11)

Supta Hasta Pādāṅguṣṭhāsana **Supta Pārśvasahita**

Inhale (12) Exhale (13) Inhale (14) Exhale (15) Inhale (16) Exhale + 5 Breaths (17) Inhale (18) Exhale + 5 Breaths (19)

Supta Hasta Pādāṅguṣṭhāsana **Supta Pārśvasahita**

Inhale (20) Exhale (21) Inhale (22) Exhale (23) Inhale Exhale (24) Inhale (25) Exhale (26)...

Chakrāsana

...Exhale (6) Inhale... Inhale (7) Exhale In. + Ex. (8) In. + 5 Br. + Ex. (9) Inhale (10) Exhale (11) Inhale (12) Exhale (13)...

Ubhaya Pādāṅguṣṭhāsana

...Exhale (6) Inhale... Inhale (7) Exhale In. + Ex. (8) Inhale (9) Ex. + 5 Br. (10) In. + Ex. (11) In. (12) Exhale (13) Inhale (14) Exhale (15)...

Ūrdhva Mukha Paśchimottānāsana

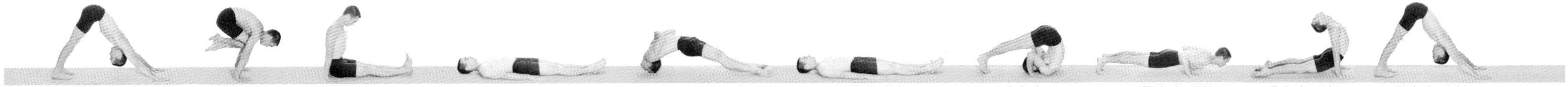

...Exhale (6) Inhale... Inhale (7) Exhale (8) Inhale + 5 Breaths (9) Exhale (10) Inhale Exhale (11) Inhale (12) Exhale (13)...

Setu Bandhāsana **Chakrāsana**

INTERMEDIATE VINYĀSA

...Exhale (6) | Inhale... | In. + 5 Breaths + Ex. (7) **Pāśāsana** | In. + 5 Breaths + Ex. (8) **Pāśāsana** | Inhale (9) | Exhale (10) | Inhale (11) | Exhale (12)...

...Exhale (6) | Inhale... | Inhale (7) | Ex. + 5 Br. (8) **Krounchāsana** | In. + Ex. (9) | Inhale (10)... **Vinyāsa** (jump back) | Inhale (14) | Ex. + 5 Br. (15) **Krounchāsana** | In. + Ex. (16) | Inhale (17) | Exhale (18) | Inhale (19) | Exhale (20)...

...Inhale (full vinyāsa optional) | Exhale (4) | Inhale + 5 Breaths (5) **Śalabhāsana A** | Exhale + 5 Breaths **Śalabhāsana B** | Inhale (6) | Exhale + Inhale (7) (full vinyāsa optional) | Exhale (4) | In. + 5 Br. + Ex. (5) **Bhekāsana** | Inhale (6) | Exhale (7)...

...Inhale (full vinyāsa optional) | Exhale (4) | In. + 5 Br. + Ex. (5) **Dhanurāsana** | Inhale (6) | Exhale + Inhale (7) | Exhale (4) | In. (5) | Ex. + 5 Br. (6) | In. (7) | Ex. + 5 Br. (8) | In. + 5 Br. + Ex. (9) **Pārśva Dhanurāsana** ☞ | In. (10) | Exhale (11)...

...Exhale (6) | Inhale (7) | Exhale + 5 Breaths (8) **Uṣṭrāsana** | Inhale + Exhale (9) | Inhale (10) | Exhale (11) | Inhale (12) | Exhale (13)...

...Exhale (6) | Inhale (7) | Exhale + 5 Breaths (8) **Laghu Vajrāsana** | Inhale... | Exhale (9) | Inhale (10) | Exhale (11) | Inhale (12) | Exhale (13)...

...Exhale (6) | Inhale (7) | Exhale + 5 Breaths (8) **Kapotāsana A** | In. + 5 Br. + Ex. (8) **Kapotāsana B** | Inhale + Exhale (9) | Inhale (10) | Exhale (11) | Inhale (12) | Exhale (13)...

...Exhale (6) | Inhale... | Inhale (7) | Ex. + In. (8) | Ex. + 5 Breaths (9) **Supta Vajrāsana** | Inhale Up & down x5 | Ex. + 5 Breaths | In. + Ex. | Inhale (10) | Exhale (11) | Inhale (12) | Exhale (13)...

...Exhale (6) | Inhale... | In. + 5 Br. + Ex. (7) **Bakāsana A** | In. (8) | Exhale (9) | Inhale (10) | Exhale (11/6) | Inhale... | In. + 5 Br. + Ex. (7) **Bakāsana B** | In. (8) | Exhale (9) | Inhale (10) | Exhale (11)...

...Exhale (6) | Inhale... | Inhale (7) | Ex. + 5 Br. (8) **Bharadvajāsana** | Inhale (9)... **Vinyāsa** (jump back) | Inhale (13) | Ex. + 5 Br. (14) **Bharadvajāsana** | Inhale (15) | Exhale (16) | Inhale (17) | Exhale (18)...

...Exhale (6) | Inhale... | Inhale (7) | Ex. + 5 Br. (8) **Ardha Matsyendrāsana** | Inhale (9)... **Vinyāsa** (jump back) | Inhale (13) | Ex. + 5 Br. (14) **Ardha Matsyendrāsana** | Inhale (15) | Exhale (16) | Inhale (17) | Exhale (18)...

...Exhale (6) | Inhale... | Inhale (7) | Exhale + 5 Breaths (8) **Eka Pāda Śīrṣāsana** | Inhale + Exhale (9) | Inhale (10) | Exhale (11) | Inhale (12) | Exhale (13)...

...Exhale (13) | Inhale... | Inhale (14) | Exhale + 5 Breaths (15) **Eka Pāda Śīrṣāsana** | Inhale + Exhale (16) | Inhale (17) | Exhale (18) | Inhale (19) | Exhale (20)...

...Exhale (6) | Inhale (7) | Exhale + 5 Breaths (8) **Dwi Pāda Śīrṣāsana** | Inhale + 5 Breaths (9) | Exhale (10) | Inhale (11) | Exhale (12)...

...Exhale (6) | Inhale... | Inhale (7) | Exhale | Inhale | Exhale + 5 Breaths (8) **Yoga Nidrāsana** | Inhale **Chakrāsana** | Exhale (9) | Inhale (10) | Exhale (11)...

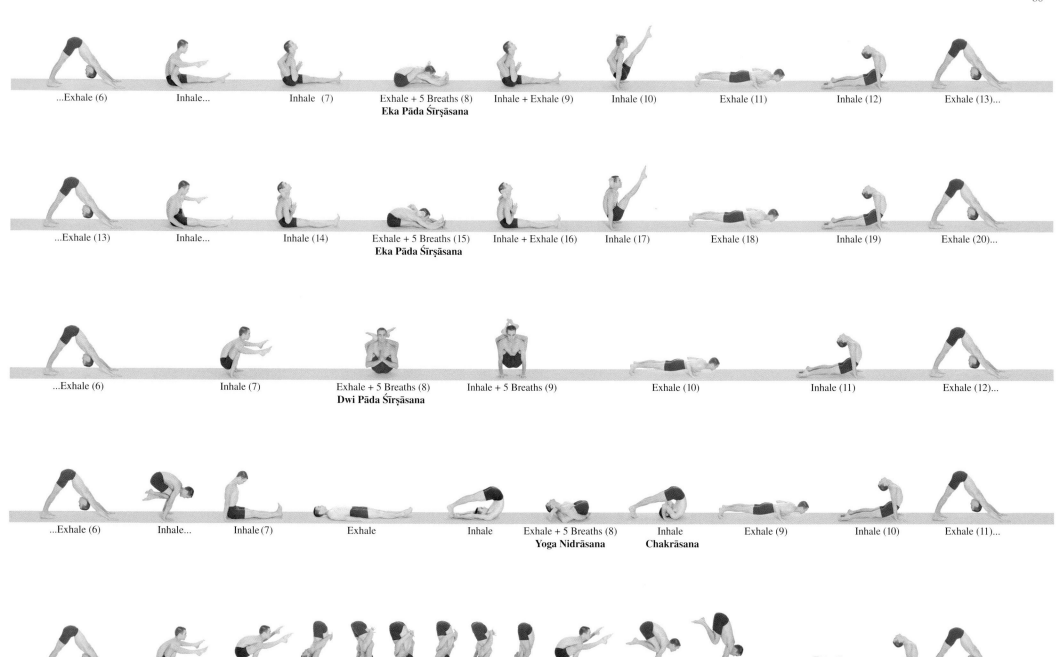

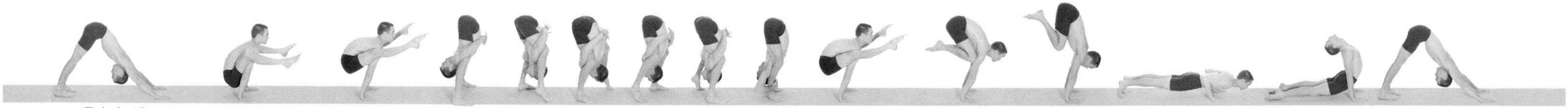

...Exhale (6) | Inhale... | In. + 5 Br. (7) **Tittibhāsana A** | Ex. + 5 Br. (8) **B** | Inhale... | Walk x5 ☞ | x5 ☜ | Ex. + 5 Br. (9) **C** | In. + 5 Br. (10) | (Exhale) | Inhale (11) | Exhale (12) | Inhale (13) | Exhale (14)...

...Exhale (6) | Inhale (7) | Exhale | Inhale + 5 Breaths (8) | Exhale (9) | Inhale (10) | Exhale (11)...

Pincha Mayūrāsana

...Exhale (6) | Inhale (7) | Exhale | Inhale (8) | Exhale... | Ex. + 5 Br. (9) | Inhale... | Inhale (10) | Exhale (11) | Inhale (12) | Exhale (13) | In. (14) | Ex. (15) | Inhale

Karandavāsana

Exhale | Inhale (1) | Exhale (2) | Inhale (3) | Exhale (4) | In. + 5 Br. + Ex. (5) | Inhale (6) | Exhale (7) | Inhale (8) | Exhale (9) | Inhale

Mayūrāsana

Exhale | In. (1) | Ex. (2) | In. (3) | Exhale (4) | Inhale (5) | Inhale | Exhale | Exhale | Inhale (6) | Exhale (7) | In. (8) | Ex. (9) | Inhale

Nakrāsana Hop x5 ☞ x5 ☜

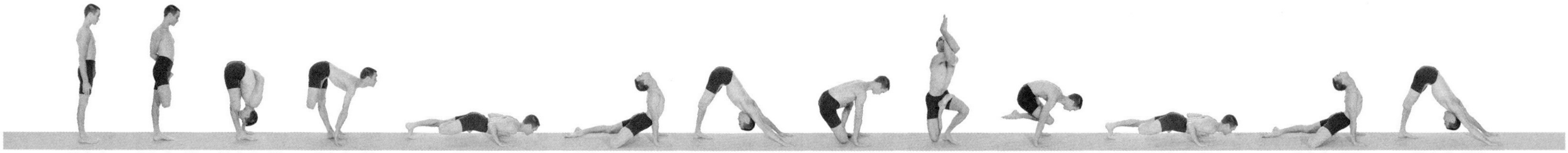

Exhale Inhale (1) Exhale (2) Inhale (3) Exhale (4) Inhale (5) Exhale (6) Inhale... In. + 5 Br. + Ex. (7) Inhale (8) Exhale (9) Inhale (10) Exhale (11)

Vātāyanāsana

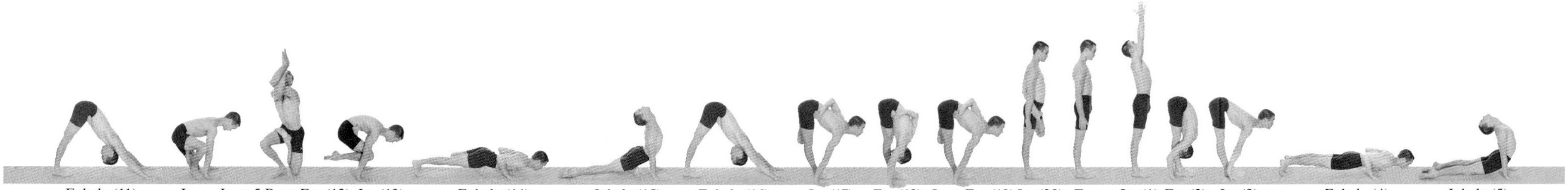

Exhale (11) In.... In. + 5 Br. + Ex. (12) In. (13) Exhale (14) Inhale (15) Exhale (16) In. (17) Ex. (18) In. + Ex. (19) In. (20) Ex. In. (1) Ex. (2) In. (3) Exhale (4) Inhale (5)

Vātāyanāsana

Exhale (6) Inhale... Inhale (7) Exhale + 5 Br. (8) In. + Ex. (9) Inhale (10)... In. (14) Ex. + 5 Br. (15) In. + Ex. (16) In. (17) Exhale (18) Inhale (19) Exhale (20)...

Parighāsana **Vinyāsa** (jump back) **Parighāsana**

...Exhale (6) Inhale (7) In. + 5 Br. (8) Ex. + 5 Br. (9) Inhale (10)... In. + 5 Br. (15) Ex. + 5 Br. (16) Inhale (17) Exhale (18) Inhale (19) Exhale (20)...

Gomukhāsana A **B** **Vinyāsa** **Gomukhāsana A** **B**

...Exhale (6) Inhale... Inhale (7) Exhale In. + Ex. (8) In. + 5 Br. + Ex. (9) Inhale (10) Exhale (11) Inhale (12) Exhale (13)...

Supta Ūrdhva Pāda Vajrāsana

...Exhale (13) Inhale... Inhale (14) Exhale In. + Ex. (15) In. + 5 Br. + Ex. (16) Inhale (17) Exhale (18) Inhale (19) Exhale (20)...

Supta Ūrdhva Pāda Vajrāsana

...Exhale (6) Inhale (7) Exhale In. + 5 Br. (8) Exhale In. + 5 Br. (8) Exhale In. + 5 Br. (8) Exhale (9) Inhale (10) Exhale (11)...

Mukta Hasta Śīrṣāsana A, B & C ☞ **Vinyāsa (Chaturāṅga)** **Vinyāsa (Chaturāṅga)** **Chaturāṅga**

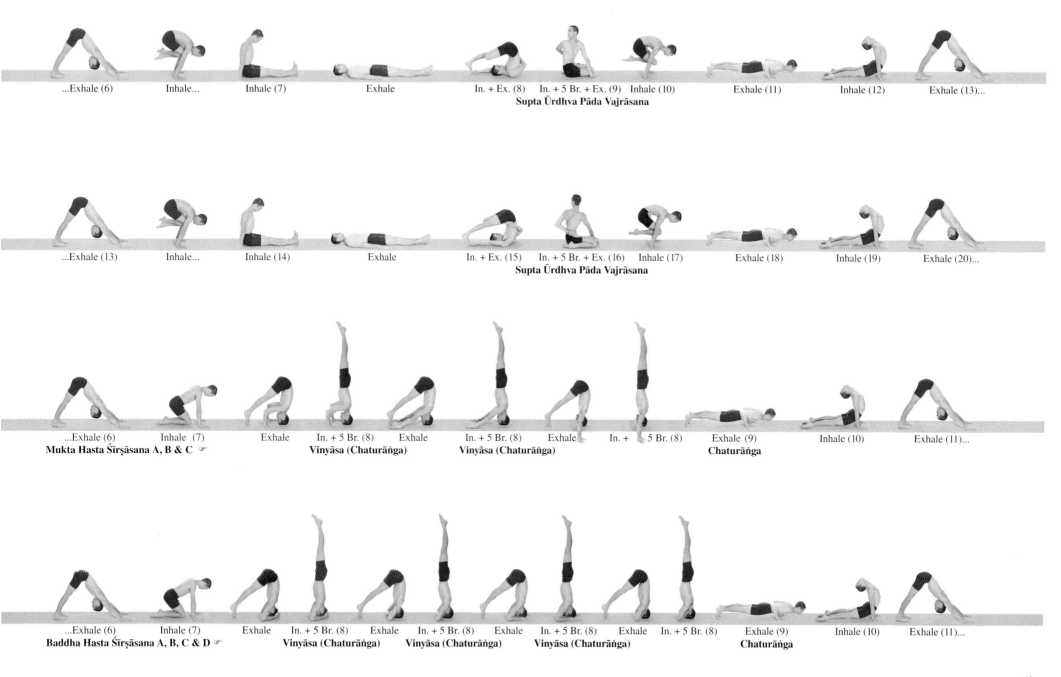

...Exhale (6) Inhale (7) Exhale In. + 5 Br. (8) Exhale In. + 5 Br. (8) Exhale In. + 5 Br. (8) Exhale In. + 5 Br. (8) Exhale (9) Inhale (10) Exhale (11)...

Baddha Hasta Śīrṣāsana A, B, C & D ☞ **Vinyāsa (Chaturāṅga)** **Vinyāsa (Chaturāṅga)** **Vinyāsa (Chaturāṅga)** **Chaturāṅga**

ADVANCED A VINYĀSA

...Exhale (6) | Inhale + Exhale (7) | Inhale + 5 Breaths (8) **Vasiṣṭhāsana** | Exhale + Inhale (9) | Exhale (10) | Inhale (11) | Exhale (12)...

...Exhale (12) | Inhale + Exhale (13) | Inhale + 5 Breaths (14) **Vasiṣṭhāsana** | Exhale + Inhale (15) | Exhale (16) | Inhale (17) | Exhale (18)...

...Exhale (6) | Inhale + 5 Breaths (7) **Viśwāmitrāsana** | Exhale (8) | Inhale (9) | Exhale (10) | Inhale (11) | Exhale (12)...

...Exhale (12) | Inhale + 5 Breaths (13) **Viśwāmitrāsana** | Exhale (14) | Inhale (15) | Exhale (16) | Inhale (17) | Exhale (18)...

...Exhale (6) | Inhale... | Inhale (7) | Exhale + 5 Breaths (8) **Kaśyapāsana** | Inhale + Exhale (9) | Inhale (10) | Exhale (11) | Inhale (12) | Exhale (13)...

...Exhale (13) Inhale... Inhale (14) Exhale + 5 Breaths (15) Inhale + Exhale (16) Inhale (17) Exhale (18) Inhale (19) Exhale (20)...

Kaśyapāsana

...Exhale (6) Inhale... In. + Ex. (7) In. + 5 Br. + Ex. (8) In. (9)... Inhale... In. + Ex. (13) In. + 5 Br. + Ex. (14) In. (15) Exhale (16) Inhale (17) Exhale (18)...

Chakorāsana **Vinyāsa** (jump back) **Chakorāsana**

...Exhale (6) In. + Ex. (7) Inhale... In. + 5 Br. (8) Exhale (9) Inhale (10)... In. + Ex. (14) Inhale... In. + 5 Br. (15) Exhale (16) Inhale (17) Exhale (18) Inhale (19) Exhale (20)...

Bhairavāsana **Vinyāsa** (jump back) **Bhairavāsana**

...Exhale (6) Inhale... In. + Ex. (7) Inhale Ex. + 5 Br. (8) In. (9)... Inhale... In. + Ex. (13) Inhale Ex. + 5 Br. (14) In. (15) Exhale (16) Inhale (17) Exhale (18)...

Skandāsana **Vinyāsa** (jump back) **Skandāsana**

...Exhale (6) In. + Ex. (7) Inhale... In. + 5 Br. + Ex. (8) In. (9)... In. + Ex. (13) Inhale... In. + 5 Br. + Ex. (14) In. (15) Exhale (16) Inhale (17) Exhale (18)...

Dūrvāsāsana **Vinyāsa** (jump back) **Dūrvāsāsana**

...Exhale (6) | Inhale (7) | Exhale (8) | In. + 5 Br. + Ex. (9) | Inhale (10) | Exhale (11) | Inhale (12) | Exhale (13)...

Ūrdhva Kukkuṭāsana A

...Exhale (6) | Inhale... | Inhale (7) | Exhale (8) | Inhale... | Inhale + 5 Breaths (9) | Exhale (10) | Inhale (11) | Exhale (12)...

Ūrdhva Kukkuṭāsana B

...Exhale (6) | Inhale... | Inhale (7) | Exhale (8) | Inhale + 5 Breaths (9) | Exhale (10) | Inhale (11) | Exhale (12)...

Ūrdhva Kukkuṭāsana C

...Exhale (6) | Inhale (7) | Exhale (8) | In. + 5 Br. + Ex. (9) | Inhale (10) | Exhale (11) | In. + 5 Br. + Ex. (12) | Inhale (13) | Exhale (14) | Inhale (15) | Exhale (16)...

Gālavāsana **Gālavāsana**

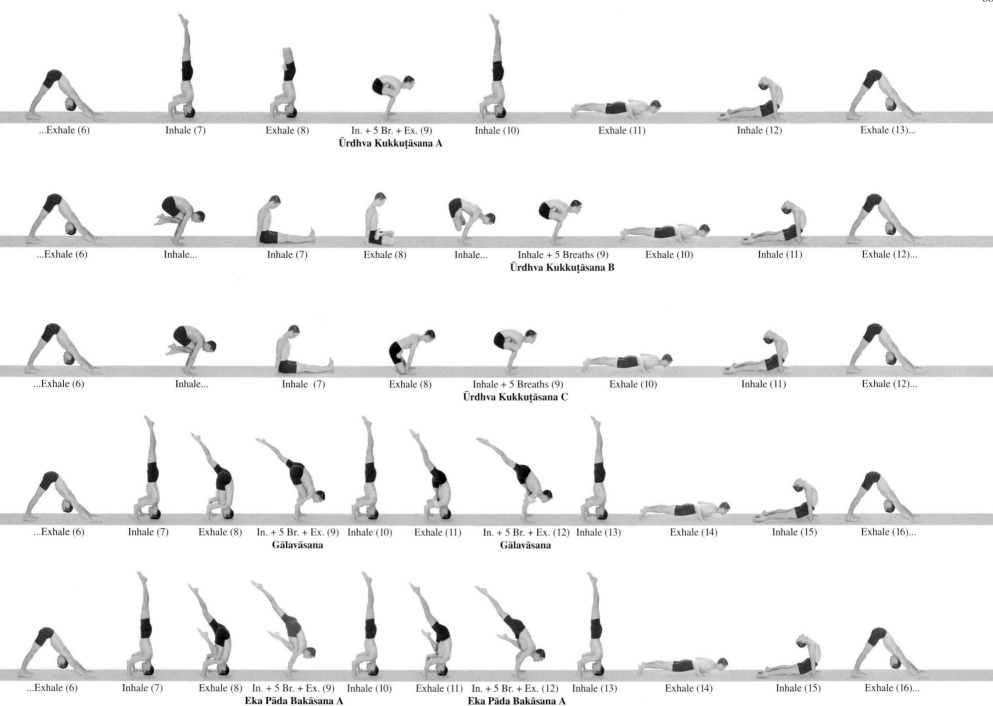

...Exhale (6) | Inhale (7) | Exhale (8) | In. + 5 Br. + Ex. (9) | Inhale (10) | Exhale (11) | In. + 5 Br. + Ex. (12) | Inhale (13) | Exhale (14) | Inhale (15) | Exhale (16)...

Eka Pāda Bakāsana A **Eka Pāda Bakāsana A**

...Exhale (6) Inhale (7) Exhale (8) In. + 5 Br. + Ex. (9) Inhale (10) Exhale (11) In. + 5 Br. + Ex. (12) Inhale (13) Exhale (14) Inhale (15) Exhale (16)...

Eka Pāda Bakāsana B **Eka Pāda Bakāsana B**

...Exhale (6) Inhale (7) Exhale (8) In. + 5 Br. + Ex. (9) Inhale (10) Exhale (11) In. + 5 Br. + Ex. (12) Inhale (13) Exhale (14) Inhale (15) Exhale (16)...

Kouṇḍinyāsana A **Kouṇḍinyāsana A**

...Exhale (6) Inhale (7) Exhale (8) In. + 5 Br. + Ex. (9) Inhale (10) Exhale (11) In. + 5 Br. + Ex. (12) Inhale (13) Exhale (14) Inhale (15) Exhale (16)...

Kouṇḍinyāsana B **Kouṇḍinyāsana B**

...Exhale (6) Inhale (7) Exhale (8) In. + 5 Br. + Ex. (9) Inhale (10) Exhale (11) In. + 5 Br. + Ex. (12) Inhale (13) Exhale (14) Inhale (15) Exhale (16)...

Aṣṭāvakrāsana A **Aṣṭāvakrāsana A**

...Exhale (6) Inhale... In. + 5 Br. (7) Exhale (8) Inhale (9) Exhale (10) Inhale... In. + 5 Br. (11) Exhale (12) Inhale (13) Exhale (14)...

Aṣṭāvakrāsana B **Aṣṭāvakrāsana B**

...Exhale (6) Inhale... Inhale (7) Exhale + 5 Breaths (8) Inhale (9) Exhale (10) Inhale (11) Exhale (12)

Pūrṇa Matsyendrāsana

Exhale (12) Inhale... Inhale (13) Exhale + 5 Breaths (14) Inhale (15) Exhale (16) Inhale (17) Exhale (18)...

Pūrṇa Matsyendrāsana

...Exhale (6) Inhale... Inhale (7) Ex. + 5 Br. (8) In. + 5 Br. + Ex. (9) In. + 5 Br. (10) Exhale (11) Inhale (12) Exhale (13)

Viranchyāsana A ☞

Exhale (13) Inhale... Inhale (14) Ex. + 5 Br. (15) In. + 5 Br. + Ex. (16) In. + 5 Br. (17) Exhale (18) Inhale (19) Exhale (20)...

Viranchyāsana A ☞

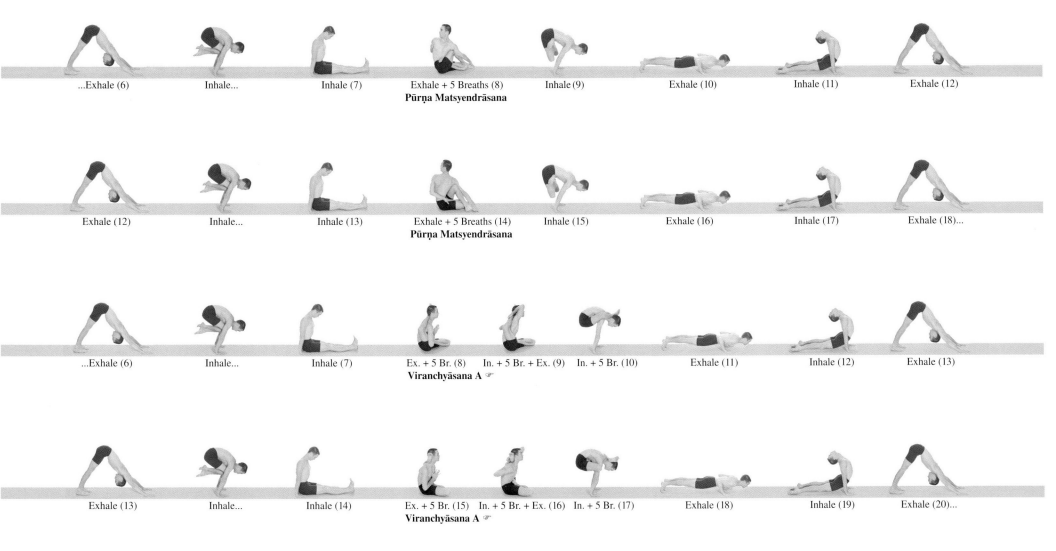

...Exhale (6) Inhale... Inhale + 5 Breaths (7) Exhale + 5 Breaths (8) Inhale (9) Ex. + 5 Br. (10) Inhale (11) Exhale (12) Inhale (13) Exhale (14)...

Viranchyāsana B ☞

...Exhale (14) | Inhale... | Inhale + 5 Breaths (15) | Exhale + 5 Breaths (16) | Inhale (17) | Ex. + 5 Br. (18) | Inhale (19) | Exhale (20) | Inhale (21) | Exhale (22)...

Viranchyāsana B ☞

...Exhale (6) | Inhale (7) | Exhale | Inhale (8) | Exhale + 5 Breaths (9) | Inhale (10) | Exhale (11) | Inhale (12) | Exhale (13)...

Viparīta Daṇḍāsana

...Exhale (6) | Inhale (7) | Exhale | Inhale (8) | Exhale (9) | In. + 5 Br. (10) | Exhale (11) | In. + 5 Br. (12) | Exhale (13) | Inhale (14) | Exhale (15) | Inhale (16) | Exhale (17)...

Eka Pāda Viparīta Daṇḍāsana ☞

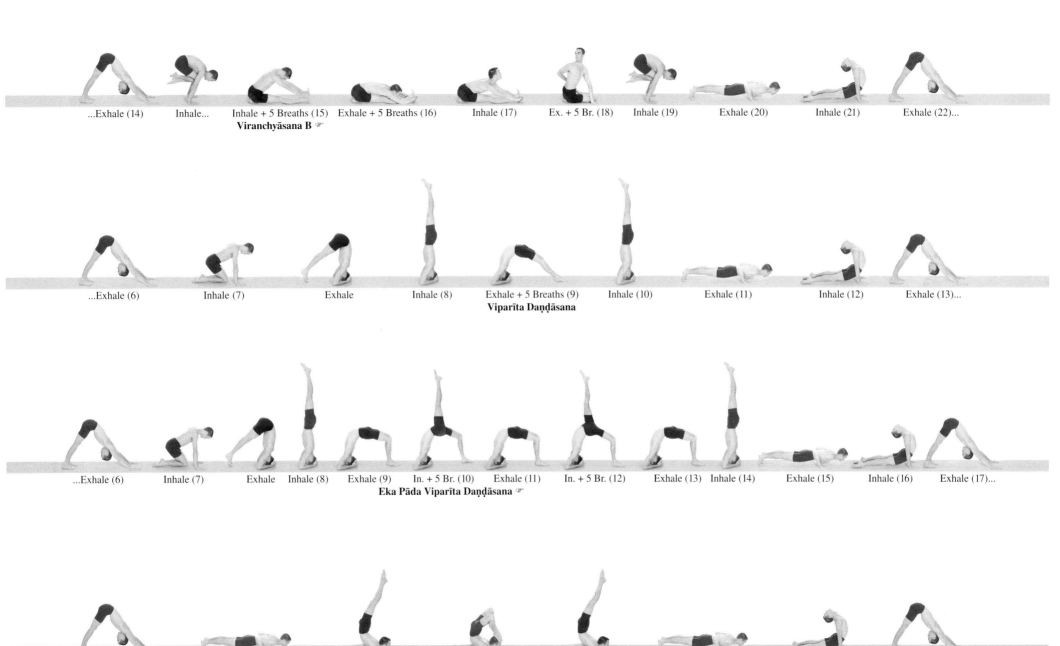

...Inhale (full vinyāsa optional) | Exhale (4) | Inhale + 5 Breaths (5) | Exhale + 5 Breaths | Inhale (5) | Exhale (6) | Inhale (7) | Exhale (8)...

Viparīta Śalabhāsana — Inhale + 5 Breaths (5)

Gaṇḍa Bheruṇḍāsana (optional) — Exhale + 5 Breaths

...Exhale (6) | Inhale... | Inhale + 5 Breaths (7) (Hands in prayer position) **A** | Exhale + 5 Breaths (8) **Hanumānāsana B** | Inhale + 5 Breaths (9) **C** | Exhale | Inhale (10) | Exhale (11) | Inhale (12) | Exhale (13)

Exhale (13) | Inhale... | Inhale + 5 Breaths (14) (Hands in prayer position) **A** | Exhale + 5 Breaths (15) **Hanumānāsana B** | Inhale + 5 Breaths (16) **C** | Exhale | Inhale (17) | Exhale (18) | Inhale (19) | Exhale (20)...

...Exhale (6) | Inhale... | Inhale (7) | Exhale | Inhale (8) | Exhale + 5 Breaths (9) **Supta Trivikramāsana** | Inhale (10) | Exhale (11)

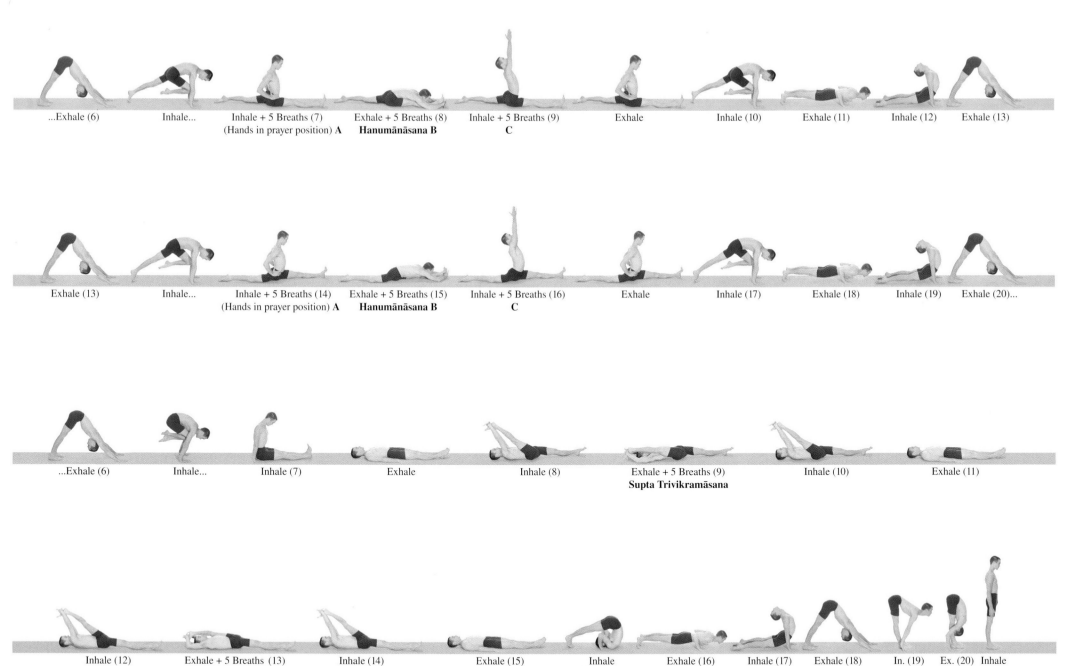

Inhale (12) | Exhale + 5 Breaths (13) **Supta Trivikramāsana** | Inhale (14) | Exhale (15) | Inhale **Chakrāsana** | Exhale (16) | Inhale (17) | Exhale (18) | In. (19) | Ex. (20) | Inhale

Exhale In. (1) Ex. (2) In. (3) Ex. + 5 Br. + In. (4) **Dīghāsana A** Ex. + 5 Br. + In. (5) **Dīghāsana B** Ex. + 5 Br. + In. (6) **Dīghāsana A** Ex. (7) In. (8) Ex. + 5 Br. + In. (9) **Dīghāsana A** Ex. + 5 Br. + In. (10) **Dīghāsana B** Ex. + 5 Br. + In. (11) **Dīghasana A** Ex. (12) Inhale

Exhale Inhale (1) Exhale + 5 Breaths (2) **Trivikramāsana** Inhale (3) Exhale Inhale (4) Exhale + 5 Breaths (5) **Trivikramāsana** Inhale (6) Exhale

Exhale Inhale (1) Exhale... Exhale + 5 Breaths (2) **Naṭarājāsana** Inhale... Inhale (3) Exhale Inhale (4) Exhale... Exhale + 5 Breaths (5) **Naṭarājāsana** Inhale... Inhale (6) Exhale

...Exhale In. (1) Ex. (2) In. (3) Exhale (4) In. + 5 Br. + Ex. (5) **Rāja Kapotāsana** Inhale (6) Exhale (7/6) (full vinyāsa optional) Inhale... Inhale (7) Ex. + 5 Br. (8) In. + Ex. (9) **Eka Pāda Rāja Kapotāsana** Inhale (10)

Exhale (11) Inhale (12) Exhale (13) Inhale... Inhale (14) Ex. + 5 Br. (15) In. + Ex. (16) **Eka Pāda Rāja Kapotāsana** Inhale (17) Exhale (18) Inhale (19) Exhale (20)...

ADVANCED B VINYĀSA

...Exhale (6) | Inhale... | Inhale (7) | Exhale + 5 Breaths (8) **Mūla Bandhāsana** | Inhale (9) | Exhale (10) | Inhale (11) | Exhale (12)...

...Exhale (6) | Inhale... | Inhale (7) | Ex. + 5 Br. + In. (8) **Nahuśāsana A** | Ex. + 5 Br. + In. (8) **B** | Ex. + 5 Br. (8) **C** | Inhale (9) | Exhale (10) | Inhale (11) | Exhale (12)...

...Exhale (6) | Inhale (7) | Exhale | Inhale (8) | Exhale + 5 Breaths (9) **Vṛśchikāsana** | Inhale (10) | Exhale (11) | Inhale (12) | Exhale (13)...

...Exhale (6) | Inhale (7) | Exhale | Inhale + 5 Breaths (8) **Śayanāsana** | Exhale (9) | Inhale (10) | Exhale (11)...

...Exhale (6) | Inhale (7) | Exhale (8) | Inhale + 5 Breaths (9) **Buddhāsana** | Inhale (10) | Exhale (11) | Inhale (12) | Exhale (13)...

...Exhale (13) | Inhale (14) | Exhale (15) | In. + 5 Br. + Ex. (16) **Buddhāsana** | Inhale (17) | Exhale (18) | Inhale (19) | Exhale (20)...

...Exhale (6) | Inhale... | Inhale (7) | Exhale + 5 Breaths (8) **Kapilāsana** | Inhale+ Exhale (9) | Inhale (10) | Exhale (11) | Inhale (12) | Exhale (13)

Exhale (13) | Inhale... | Inhale (14) | Exhale + 5 Breaths (15) **Kapilāsana** | Inhale+ Exhale (16) | Inhale (17) | Exhale (18) | Inhale (19) | Exhale (20)...

...Exhale (6) | Inhale... | Inhale (7) | Exhale (8) | In. + 5 Br. (9) **Ākarṇa Dhanurāsana A** | Ex. + 5 Br. (10) **B** | Inhale (11) | Exhale (12)

In. + 5 Br. (13) **Ākarṇa Dhanurāsana A** | Ex. + 5 Br. (14) **B** | Inhale (15) | Exhale (16) | Inhale (17) | Exhale (18) | Inhale (19) | Exhale (20)...

...Inhale (20) (full vinyāsa optional) · Exhale (4) · Inhale + 5 Breaths (5) **Pādāṅguṣṭha Dhanurāsana A** · Exhale + 5 Breaths (6) **B** · Inhale + 5 Breaths + Ex. (7) **A** · Inhale (8) · Exhale (9)...

...Exhale (6) · Inhale... · In. (7) · Ex. + 5 Br. (8) **Marīchyāsana E** · In. + Ex. (9) · Inhale (10)... **Vinyāsa** (jump back) · In. (14) · Ex. + 5 Br. (15) **Marīchyāsana E** · In. + Ex. (16) · Inhale (17) · Exhale (18) · Inhale (19) · Exhale (20)...

...Exhale (6) · Inhale... · Inhale + 5 Breaths (7) **Marīchyāsana F** · Inhale (8)... **Vinyāsa** (jump back) · Inhale + 5 Breaths (12) **Marīchyāsana F** · Inhale (13) · Exhale (14) · Inhale (15) · Exhale (16)...

...Exhale (6) · Inhale... · In. (7) · Ex. + 5 Br. (8) **Marīchyāsana G** · In. + Ex. (9) · In. (10)... **Vinyāsa** (jump back) · Inhale... · In. (14) · Ex. + 5 Br. (15) **Marīchyāsana G** · In. + Ex. (16) · In. (17) · Exhale (18) · Inhale (19) · Exhale (20)...

...Exhale (6) · Inhale... · In. + 5 Br. + Ex. (7) **Marīchyāsana H** · In. (8)... **Vinyāsa** (jump back) · Inhale... · In. + 5 Br. + Ex. (12) **Marīchyāsana H** · In. (13) · Exhale (14) · Inhale (15) · Exhale (16) · In. (17) · Ex. (18) · Inhale

Exhale In. (1) Ex. (2) In. (3) Exhale (4) Inhale (5) Exhale (6) Inhale... In. + 5 Br. + Ex. (7) In. (8) Exhale (9) Inhale (11) Exhale (12)...

Tāḍāsana

...Inhale (full vinyāsa optional) Exhale (4) Inhale + Exhale (5) Inhale + 5 Breaths (6) Exhale + Inhale (7) Exhale (8) Inhale (9) Exhale (10)

Samānāsana

...Inhale (10) Exhale (11) Inhale + Exhale (12) Inhale + 5 Breaths (13) Exhale + Inhale (14) Exhale (15) Inhale (16) Exhale (17)

Samānāsana

...Exhale (6) Inhale (7) Exhale (8) In. + 5 Br. + Ex. (9) Inhale (10) Exhale (11) In. + 5 Br. + Ex. (12) Inhale (13) Exhale (14) Inhale (15) Exhale (16)...

Pārśva Bakāsana **Pārśva Bakāsana**

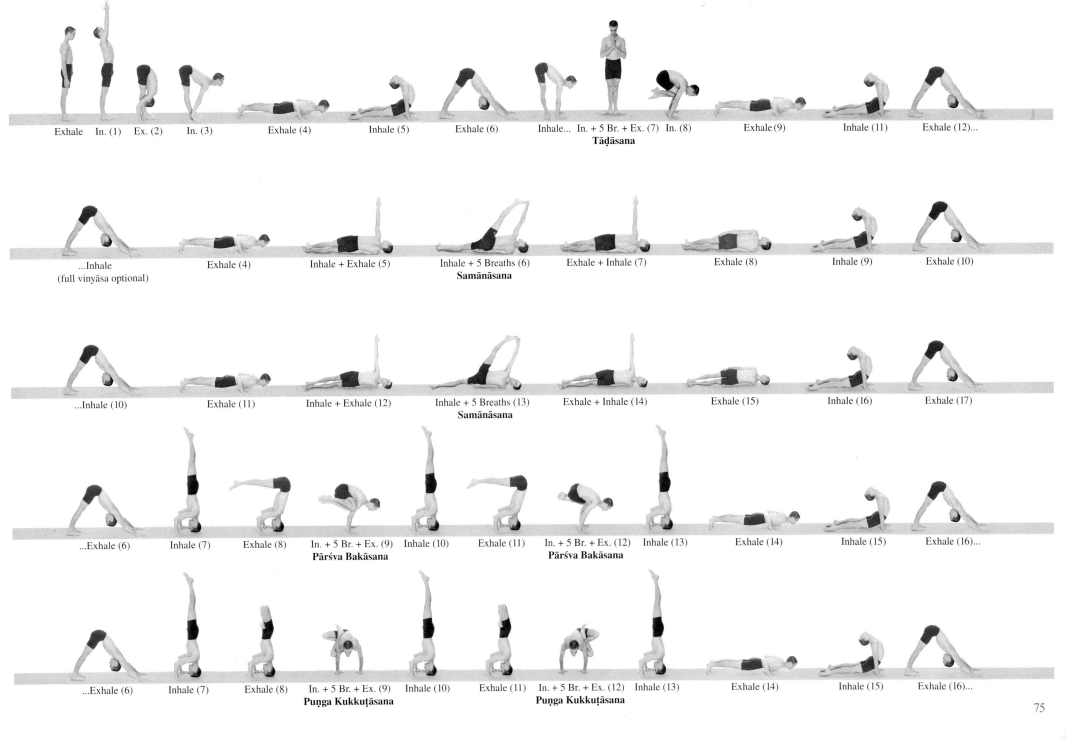

...Exhale (6) Inhale (7) Exhale (8) In. + 5 Br. + Ex. (9) Inhale (10) Exhale (11) In. + 5 Br. + Ex. (12) Inhale (13) Exhale (14) Inhale (15) Exhale (16)...

Puṇga Kukkuṭāsana **Puṇga Kukkuṭāsana**

...Inhale (16) (full vinyāsa optional)	Exhale (4)	In. + 5 Br. + Ex. (5) **Eka Pāda Dhanurāsana**	Inhale (6)	Exhale + Inhale (7)	Exhale (8)	In. + 5 Br. + Ex. (9) **Eka Pāda Dhanurāsana**	Inhale (10)	Exhale (11)...

...Exhale (6)	Inhale...	Inhale (7)	Exhale + 5 Breaths (8) **Eka Pāda Kapotāsana**	Inhale + Exhale (9)	Inhale (10)	Exhale (11)	Inhale (12)	Exhale (13)...

...Exhale (13)	Inhale...	Inhale (14)	Exhale + 5 Breaths (15) **Eka Pāda Kapotāsana**	Inhale + Exhale (16)	Inhale (17)	Exhale (18)	Inhale (19)	Exhale (20)...

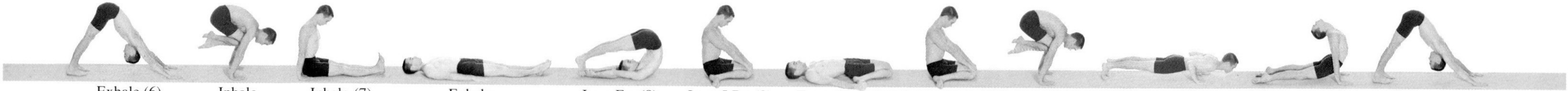

...Exhale (6)	Inhale...	Inhale (7)	Exhale	In. + Ex. (8)	In. + 5 Br. (9)	Ex. + 5 Br. (10)	In. + Ex. (11)	Inhale (12)	Exhale (13)	Inhale (14)	Exhale (15)...

Paryaṅgāsana A & B

...Exhale (6)	Inhale (7)	Exhale	Inhale (8)	Exhale + Inhale (9) **Parivrttāsana A**	Exhale Circle anti clockwise x3 (	Inhale...	...Inhale	Exhale...

...Exhale + Inhale **Parivṛttāsana A** | Exhale Circle clockwise x3 ↻ | Inhale... | ...Inhale | Exhale | Inhale (10) | Exhale (11) | Inhale (12) | Exhale 13)...

...Exhale (6) | Inhale (7) | Exhale + Inhale (8) **Parivṛttāsana B** | Exhale Circle anti clockwise x3 ↺ | Inhale... | ...Inhale | Exhale...

...Exhale + Inhale **Parivṛttāsana B** | Exhale Circle clockwise x3 ↻ | ...Inhale | ...Inhale | Exhale | Inhale (9) | Exhale (10) | Inhale (11) | Exhale (12)...

...Exhale (6) | Inhale... | Inhale (7) | Exhale + 5 Breaths (8) **Yoni Daṇḍāsana** | Inhale (9)... **Vinyāsa** (jump back) | Inhale (13) | Exhale + 5 Breaths (14) **Yoni Daṇḍāsana** | Inhale (15) | Exhale (16) | Inhale (17) | Exhale (18)...

...Exhale (6) | Inhale... | Inhale (7) | Exhale + 5 Breaths (8) **Yoga Daṇḍāsana** | Inhale (9)... **Vinyāsa** (jump back) | Inhale (13) | Exhale + 5 Breaths (14) **Yoga Daṇḍāsana** | Inhale (15) | Exhale (16) | Inhale (17) | Exhale (18)...

...Exhale (6) | Inhale (7) | Exhale + 5 Breaths (8) **Bhuja Daṇḍāsana** | Inhale (9) | Exhale (10) | Inhale (11) | Exhale (12)...

...Exhale (12) | Inhale (13) | Exhale + 5 Breaths (14) **Bhuja Daṇḍāsana** | Inhale (15) | Exhale (16) | Inhale (17) | Exhale (18)...

...Exhale (6) | Inhale... | Inhale + Exhale (7) | Inhale... | In. + 5 Br. + Ex. (8) **Pārśva Daṇḍāsana** | Inhale (9) | Exhale (10) | Inhale (11) | Exhale (12)...

...Exhale (12) | Inhale... | Inhale + Exhale (13) | Inhale... | In. + 5 Br. + Ex. (14) **Pārśva Daṇḍāsana** | Inhale (15) | Exhale (16) | Inhale (17) | Exhale (18)...

...Exhale (6) | Inhale... | Inhale + Exhale (7) | Inhale... | In. + 5 Br. + Ex. (8) **Ūrdhva Daṇḍāsana B** | Inhale (9) | Exhale (10) | Inhale (11) | Exhale (12)...

...Exhale (12) Inhale... Inhale + Exhale (13) Inhale... In. + 5 Br. + Ex. (14) Inhale (15) Exhale (16) Inhale (17) Exhale (18)...

Ūrdhva Daṇḍāsana B

...Exhale (6) Inhale (7) Ex. + 5 Br. (8) In. (9) Exhale (10) Inhale (11) Exhale (12) Inhale (13) Ex. + 5 Br. (14) In. (15) Exhale (16) Inhale (17) Exhale (18)...

Adho Daṇḍāsana **Adho Daṇḍāsana**

...Exhale (6) Inhale... Inhale (7) Exhale + 5 Breaths (8) Inhale (9) Exhale (10) Inhale (11) Exhale (12)...

Sama Koṇāsana

...Exhale (6) Inhale... Inhale + Exhale (7) Inhale... In. + 5 Br. + Ex. (8) Inhale (9) Exhale (10) Inhale (11) Exhale (12)...

Omkarāsana

...Exhale (12) Inhale... Inhale + Exhale (13) Inhale... In. + 5 Br. + Ex. (14) Inhale (15) Exhale (16) Inhale (17) Exhale (18)...

Omkarāsana

MANGALA MANTRA
"Auspicious Prayer"

OM

svasthi prajābhyaḥ paripāla yantāṁ
nyāyena mārgeṇa mahīṁ mahiśāḥ
go brāhmaṇebhyaḥ śubamastu nityaṁ
lokā samasthā sukhino bhavantu

OM

May all mankind be prosperous -
May leaders govern the world with law and justice,
May divinity and erudition be protected,
May people of the world be happy.

Glossary

abhyāsa	practice
acharya	teacher
ahimsā	non-violence
ājñā	to perceive or to command
amṛita	elixir
anāhata	unstruck
aṅga	limb
aṅguṣtha	finger or digit
antara	internal
apāna	not yet integrated
aparigraha	non-greediness
āsana	seat
aṣṭau	eight
asteya	non-stealing
ātman	individual soul
bāhya	external
bandha	lock or blockage
bandhuk	four petaled flower
bhaga	strength
bhakti	devotion or love
bindu	point or dot
Brahmā	Creator God
brahmacharya	chastity or teacher of the soul
brahmamuhurta	time of Brahmā
Brahman	universal soul
brahmaraṇdhra	hole for the soul
chakra	wheel
chatuari	four
chikitsa	therapy
chitta	mind
chitsabhā	hall of consciousness
daśā	ten
dhāraṇā	concentration
dhyāna	meditation
dośa	constitution
dṛiṣṭi	perception or looking place
dve(dwi)	two
ekam	one
ekuna	minus one
guṇa	a quality
guru	heavy one or dark/light
granthi	knot
hasta	hand
haṭha	sun and moon or forceful
iḍā	pale or blue (left/feminine)
Īśvara	God
jālandhara	net in the stream
jñāna	knowledge or wisdom
kaṅda	egg
kapha	embrace, keep together, water
karma	action
kriyā	cleansing
krama	one by one or step by step
kumbhaka	retention
kuṇḍalinī	she who is coiled
mālā	necklace or garland
maṅgala	auspicious
maṇipūraka	city of gems
mantra	mind freeing chant
mūla	root
mūlādhāra	root foundation
nabi	navel
nāḍī	nerve or conduit
nasa	nose
nauli	churning
nawa	nine
nilayam	college or abode
nirodhaḥ	cessation or restrained
niyama	personal observances
pāda	foot
pancha	five
piṅgalā	reddish (right/masculine)
pitta	heat, cook, transform, fire
prāṇa	energy or breath
prāṇāyāma	development of energy
praṇidhānani	surrender
pratyāhāra	withdrawal of the mind
pūraka	inhalation
rāja	king
rajas	activity
rechaka	exhalation
ṛiṣi	sage or saint
Rudra	incarnation of *Śiva*
sahasrāra	thousandfold
śakti	power
śala	school
samādhi	enlightenment
samāna	equalising
sannyasin	spiritual seeker or renunciate
śanti	peace
santoṣa	contentment
sapta	seven
śat	six
sattva	rhythm or tranquility
satya	truth
śaucha	cleanliness
śava	corpse
siddhi	divine attribute
Śiva	Destroyer God
śodhana	purification
sthamba	transition
sthira	steadiness
sukha	lightness
suṣumṇā	penetrating
svādhyāya	self-study
svādiṣṭhāna	sweetness
tamas	inertia
tantra	thread on the loom
tapas	self-discipline
tatsat	I am that
Trimūrti	three divines
trini	three
tristhānaṁ	three places of attention
udāna	upward moving
uḍḍīyāna	to fly up
ujjāyi	extended victory
vairāgya	detachment
vāta	wind, flow, to move, air
vāyu	air, vital force
vimsatiḥ	twenty
vini	single movement
vinyāsa	movement
vīra	hero
Viṣṇu	Preserver God
viśuddha	purity
vṛtti	fluctuation or whirlpool
vyāna	apart
yama	self restraint
yantra	to sustain
yoga	union or to yoke
yoni-mudrā	womb or female seal or awakened *kuṇḍalinī*

Āsana Index

Asana (root)	Asana (prefix)	Translation	Page
Naṭarājāsana		King *Naṭa's* posture (Lord of the Dance)	45, 71
Nāvāsana		Boat posture	41, 56
Nidrāsana	*Yoga*	*Yogi* sleeping posture	42, 60
Omkarāsana		Holy Syllable (Shape of *Om*) posture	47, 79
Pādāṅguṣṭhāsana	*Hasta*	Hand (holding) toe posture	38, 52
	Supta	Prone (holding) toe posture	41, 57
	Ubhaya	Toes together posture	41, 57
	Utthita Hasta	Upright hand (holding) toe posture	39, 53
Pādāsana	*Uttāna*	Intense outstretched foot posture	50
	Utthita Eka	Upright one foot (out) posture	39, 53
Padmāsana		Lotus flower posture	51
	Baddha	Bound lotus posture	51
	Ūrdhva	Upward lotus posture	50
Padmottānāsana	*Ardha Baddha*	Bound half-lotus stretch posture	39, 53
Pādottānāsana	*Prasārita* (A, B, C, & D)	Wide stance foot stretch posture	39, 52
Parighāsana		Twisted iron bar posture	43, 62
Paryāṅgāsana	(A & B)	Revolving limb posture	47, 76
Parivṛttāsana	(A & B)	Spinning top posture	47, 76
Pārśvasahita	*Utthita*	Upright (also to the) side	39, 53
	Supta	Prone (also to the) side	41, 57
Pārśvottānāsana	*Utthita*	Upright side stretch posture	38, 53
Pāśāsana		Noose posture	42, 58
Paśchimottānāsana	(A, B & C)	Stretched West-side posture	40, 54
	Ardha Baddha Padma	Bound half-lotus West-side posture	40, 54
	Tirieng Mukha Eka Pāda	Oblique (leg), face to foot West-side posture	40, 54
	Ūrdhva Mukha	Upward facing West-side posture	41, 57
Pīḍāsana	*Bhuja*	Arm/shoulder pressing posture	41, 56
	Karṇa	Ear pressing posture	50
Piṇḍāsana		Embryo posture	50
	Garbha	Embryo (in the) womb posture	41, 56
Pūrvottānāsana		Stretched East-side posture	40, 54
Śalabhāsana	(A & B)	Grasshopper posture	42, 58
	Viparīta	Inverted grasshopper posture	45, 69
Samānāsana		Straight/balanced posture	46, 75
Samasthitiḥ		Straight balanced upright	36, 52
Sarvāṅgāsana	*Salamba*	All limbs supported posture	50
Śayanāsana		Couch (*yogi* reclining) posture	46, 72
Śīrṣāsana		Head (stand) posture	51
	Baddha Hasta (A, B, C & D)	Bound hands (in) headstand	43, 63
	Mukta Hasta (A, B & C)	Free hands (in) headstand	43, 63
	Jānu (A, B & C)	Head (to) knee posture	40, 54
	Dwi Pāda	Two feet (behind) head posture	42, 60
	Eka Pāda	One foot (behind) head posture	42, 60
Skandāsana		God of war (*Skanda's*) posture	44, 65
Sūryanamaskara	(A & B)	Salute to the sun	36
Śvānāsana	*Adho Mukha*	Downward facing dog posture	36
	Ūrdhva Mukha	Upward facing dog posture	36
Tāḍāsana		Mountain posture	46, 75
Tittibhāsana	(A, B & C)	Firefly posture	42, 60
Trivikramāsana		Three steps (long stride of *Viṣṇu*) posture	45, 71
	Supta	Prone three steps posture	45, 70
Uṣṭrāsana		Camel posture	42, 58
Utkaṭasana		Powerful posture	39, 53
Utpluthiḥ		Uprooted	51
Uttānāsana	(A & B)	Stretched forward posture	36
Vajrāsana	*Laghu*	Short thunderbolt posture	42, 59
	Supta	Prone (long) thunderbolt posture	42, 59
	Supta Ūrdhva Pāda	Prone face-up to foot thunderbolt posture	43, 63
Vasiṣṭhāsana		Sage *Vasiṣṭha's* posture	44, 64
Vātāyanāsana		Horse posture	43, 62
Vīrabhadrāsana	(A & B)	Hero-warrior posture	39, 53
Viranchyāsana	(A & B)	Sage *Viranchi's* posture	45, 68
Viśwamitrasana		Sage *Viśwamitra's* posture	34, 64
Vṛkṣāsana		Tree (handstand) posture	48
	Ūrdhva	Upward tree posture	36
Vṛśchikāsana	(A)	Scorpion posture	46, 72
	(B)		49

Bibliography

Bowen, P.G., *The Sayings of the Ancient One.*
Theosophical Publishing House, U.S.A., 1970.

Buddhananda, Chela, *Moola Bandha: The Master Key.*
Bihar School of Yoga, Bihar, India, 1984.

Chandra Vasu, Śrisa Bahadur, *The Gheranda Samhita.*
Sri Satguru Publications, New Delhi, 1986.

Chandra Vasu, Śrisa Rai Bahadur, *The Śiva Samhita.*
Śri Satguru Publications, New Delhi, 1984.

Desikachar, T.K.V., *The Yoga Sutras of Patanjali.*
Affiliated East West Press, Madras, 1987.

Desikachar, T.K.V., *The Yoga of T. Krishnamacharya.*
Krishnamacharya Yoga Mandiram, Madras, 1987.

Gibran, Kahlil, *The Prophet.*
Alfred A. Knopf, Inc., New York, 1981.

Hesse, Herman, *Siddhartha.*
Bantham Books, New York, 1971.

Iyengar, B.K.S., *The Yoga Sutras of Patanjali.*
Harper Collins Publishers, New Delhi, 1993.

Jois, K.P., *Yoga Mala.*
North Point Press, New York, 2002.

Chia, Mantak & Maneewan, *Healing Love Through Tao, Cultivating Female Sexual Energy.*
Universal Tao Publications, New Jersey, 1991.

Chia, Mantak and Winn, Michael, *Taoist Secrets of Love, Cultivating Male Sexual Energy.*
Aurora Press, Santa Fe, 1984.

Miele, Lino, *Ashtanga Yoga, Series I & II.*
Via Cassia 698, 00189 Rome, Italy, 1996.

Sinh, Panchah, *The Hatha Yoga Pradipika,*
Sri Satguru Publications, New Delhi, 1991.

Śivananda, Swami, *The Science of Pranayama.*
The Divine Life Society, Himalayas, 1993.

Subramuniyaswami, Satguru Sivaya, *Dancing with Siva.*
Himalayan Acadamy, USA, 1993.

Sweeney, Matthew, *Chandra Moon Sequence.*
Self published poster, www.yogatemple.biz, 2005.

Vamana Rishi, *The Yoga Korunta.*
No publication known.

About the Author:

I first became interested in martial arts at the age of ten after seeing Star Wars. I wanted to be a Jedi Knight and have a teacher like Obiwan Kenobi or Master Yoda. I studied various disciplines over a fourteen year period, accumulating two black-belts and one brown-belt. As a teenager I was introduced to *yoga* by my martial arts teacher. In my twenties I studied Shiatsu therapy, skeletal adjustments, corrective exercise, *Oki yoga, Iyengar yoga, Aṣṭāṅga yoga* and macrobiotics.

Eventually my principle focus became *Aṣṭāṅga yoga* and meditation. It has been the practice that has consistently inspired me, even when my energy was flagging. More recently my interests have included different approaches to meditation, including Gestalt therapy and transpersonal therapy. Just as I value certain *āsana* and meditation techniques above others, I value these above other forms of therapy. It is something I can recommend to all practitioners of *yogāsana*.

My first *Aṣṭāṅga* teacher was Trevor Tangye and after a few years of practicing *Aṣṭāṅga* I went to Mysore. Pattabhi Jois imparted qualities of quietness, intense focus and a sense of humour about the practice. The Mysore method contributed greatly to my focus, it helped to define my strengths and weaknesses. After going to Mysore I felt I had absorbed an aspect of the tradition, call it living history, that I had not really grasped before. I call Pattabhi Jois "Guruji" with great affection, but the truth is, he is one of my teachers. Love is there, but the true Guru/Disciple relationship is an esoteric one and presently beyond me.

After some years of practice my motivation changed again, I wanted to convey the *yoga* to others. It is only after years of teaching that I wonder at that peculiar desire: does teaching hinder or help an individual's development? Yet teaching *yoga* is a gift, and it is work alone that is one's privilege.

May the force be with you

Matthew Sweeney